*It is a tale of love that transcends time  
and captures the hearts of all who hear it...*

# Dancing in Darkness

A Teenage Mother's Journey of Resilience,  
Self-Discovery, and Love

**Prof. Jerushia McDonald-Hylton**

Prof. Jerushia McDonald-Hylton's book titles may be purchased in bulk for educational, ministerial, business, fundraising, or sales promotion use. For more information, please email jerushiaunscripted@gmail.com, +1 (702) 587-6430, https:www.nwlvfs.com.

Instagram: @Jerushia_unscripted_unplugged

**Printed in the United States of America**

*Published by*

**YPN Publishing and Media, LLC**
*Leading International Publishing and Media Group*
30 N Gould Street, Sheridan, WY 82801 USA
3A/2B Kano Crescent Agbara Estate, LA, NG

Mobile: +2348023768604
Email: admin@ypnpublishers-media.com
Web: www.ypnpublishers-media.com

 @ypnpublishers
 @ypnpublishers
 Ypnpublishingmedia

# DEDICATION

This book is a heartfelt dedication to teenage mothers who have faced fear and uncertainty while navigating the challenging path of motherhood. It serves as a reminder that, despite the obstacles, life is full of opportunities to dream big and create a bright future for yourself and your child. Through my own experiences, I aim to inspire and uplift you, showing that dreams can indeed come true and that you have the strength to live your best life. Whether you are at a crossroads in life or seeking solace and resilience, this book is a beacon of hope, guiding you toward self-discovery and the realization that love has the power to transform and heal. May this story encourage you to embrace your inner strength, discover hidden treasures within yourself, and share the message of hope with others.

I dedicate this book to my beloved daughter, Patrina McDonald, also known as Patrina Wisdom. Patrina, my Love Child, came into my life when I was just 16 years old, and she has been the beacon of light that has guided me ever since. Her beautiful smile and the love shining through her big green eyes have been my source of strength and hope during the most challenging moments of my journey as a young mother. Through her, I have learned that love has the incredible power to uplift and empower us, enabling us to persevere and thrive.

I also dedicate this book to the precious blessings that Patrina has brought into my life—my four grandchildren: Jordan, Ramsey, Ajani, and Taycuan Hakbar, as well as our newest family member, my great-granddaughter, Jewel Thompson.

# ACKNOWLEDGMENT

This book is dedicated to my encouraging partner, Anthony Hylton, whose unwavering support, love, and encouragement have been the driving force behind my journey. With his uplifting words and steadfast belief in me, Anthony has been a great source of strength and motivation, inspiring me to pursue my dreams and reach new heights. Thank you for being my rock, my cheerleader, and my guiding light. Your presence in my life has made all the difference, and I am grateful for your unwavering support every step of the way.

To Suziliene, Paula, Maria, Tracy McDonald, Summer and Keith Allen, Paige Sagal, Lisa Archie, Dawn, Pastor Allen, Debra and Carol Pope, Alisa Howard, and all my spiritual daughters from around the globe: I want you all to know how deeply grateful I am for your unwavering love and support. Your encouragement and belief in me have been a driving force in my pursuit of writing this book. Your presence in my life, whether through reading my scripts or offering words of encouragement, has been a source of strength during my most challenging moments. I am forever thankful for each one of you standing by my side. Thank you for being my rock and for believing in me wholeheartedly. Your unwavering support and love have been a beacon of light in my life, and I am truly blessed to have you all by my side.

I want to express my deepest gratitude for everything you have done for me. Your unwavering support helped me overcome challenges and achieve the milestone of getting my book published. Your role in my journey cannot be understated, and I want to sincerely thank you all from the bottom of my heart. I love each of you, and I pray that God blesses you abundantly.

I also want to acknowledge my husband, whom I lovingly refer to as Papa Bear. He believed in me when I struggled to believe in myself, offering both encouragement and financial support. He has a special gift from above—the ability to see the good in everyone and provide unwavering support. Papa Bear, you are a gentle giant in my life, and I am forever grateful for your love and belief in me. Thank you for seeing my potential and choosing me as your partner and wife. I love you deeply and eternally.

To my dear friend and Pastor, Pastor Allen, I want to express my heartfelt thanks for your encouragement and mentorship. You helped me step out of my comfort zone and share my personal story with the world. Your support has been indispensable in keeping me focused on my goal of publishing this book. I cannot express enough gratitude for your presence in my life; you are a hidden gem sent by God to guide me out of darkness and into a brighter future. Your wisdom, guidance, and friendship are priceless to me, and I will always cherish the impact you have had on my life.

Thank you for everything you have done for me.

To my beloved children and grandchildren, you are my source of inspiration and joy. Your understanding, patience, and constant encouragement have been instrumental in the realization of this project. Your unwavering belief in my dreams fuels my determination, and I am forever grateful for your unwavering support.

I extend my heartfelt gratitude to the exceptional team at YPN Publishing & Media, LLC. Your expertise in editing, design, and publishing has been crucial in refining the ideas within this book. Your commitment to excellence and ability to bring concepts to life in impactful ways are truly commendable. Thank you for your dedication and hard work.

I am deeply thankful to all the wonderful friends and family members who have contributed to the success of this book. Your support, encouragement, and constructive feedback have been invaluable. Each of you has played a unique and significant role in shaping this work, and I am grateful for your contributions.

A special thank you goes to Nina Yang Shaw for her exceptional artistic contribution to this project. The stunning cover painting, titled "IRIS," created in oil on canvas with dimensions of 6ft. x 4ft., is not just a visual adornment but a profound representation of the themes woven into the narrative. We appreciate Nina's creative brilliance and recognize her work, which has not only enhanced the cover but has become an integral part of the essence of this book. Thank you, Nina, for your incredible talent and contribution.

For copyright purposes, the artistic expression captured in "IRIS" stands as a testament to Nina Yang Shaw's talent and dedication. We express our heartfelt thanks for her invaluable contribution, enriching the visual experience and encapsulating the essence of this tale within the strokes of her artistic mastery.

A sincere thank you to God Almighty and the Holy Spirit for guiding me, providing strength during challenging times, and blessing me with the creativity and insight necessary to convey the messages within these pages.

May this book embody the collective spirit of love, faith, and camaraderie that surrounds me. Your presence in my life has enriched this journey, and I feel truly blessed to have each of you by my side.

# PREFACE

Love is a force; one that effortlessly traverses boundaries and challenges the limitations of expectation. Its enchanting essence weaves its magic into the unlikeliest corners of our lives, entwining itself within the fabric of our existence. Within these pages lies the captivating tale of "Dancing in Darkness," where love, resilience, and the pursuit of self-discovery form the intricate threads of an extraordinary narrative.

At its heart, this story pulsates with the life of Olivette, a young teenage mother perched at life's crossroads, delicately balancing her responsibilities against the yearning for an elusive escape.

She embarks on a journey of transformation with the help of music's rhythm, the allure of the dimly lit dance floor, and the captivating mystery of the unknown. Within the pulse of the dance, the whispers of a dream, and the fragrance of a solitary leaf, she finds her pathway to love and self-realization.

As Olivette takes her first step into the night, she surrenders herself to the beauty of an enchanting world awaiting her arrival. It becomes her sanctuary, a fleeting haven where the burdens of life are left outside its walls. The magical allure of love is like a spellbinding melody, captivating hearts and souls with its irresistible charm. It weaves a tapestry of emotions that transcend time and space, binding two souls in an unbreakable bond.

Love's enchantment is a force that ignites passion, kindles hope, and inspires the deepest of emotions. It is a journey of discovery, a dance of vulnerability and strength, a path that leads to self-realization and profound connection. In the embrace of love's enchantment, we find solace, joy, and the beauty of shared experiences that illuminate our lives with a radiant glow.

This narrative unfolds as an exploration of the enduring power of love, resilience, and self-discovery. It calls upon the reader to embrace the dance of love in their own lives, encouraging them to uncover the hidden treasures within themselves and to spread the message of love and empathy to the world.

"Dancing in Darkness" serves as a reminder that even in the darkest moments, a glimmer of hope always persists. Love serves as a guiding light, a treasure waiting to be found within each of us.

The story mirrors the journey of a mother, a dreamer, and a lover who carved her own path, navigated life's complexities, and created a future that defied all expectations.

So, settle in and enjoy this captivating journey. May the upcoming chapters inspire you to dance to the rhythm of your heart, discover the treasures within, and share the transformative power of love with the world.

# FOREWORD I

If you're seeking a revelation in your life and yearn to uncover the unwavering rhythm that dances alongside you, brace yourself!

Professor Jerushia has masterfully unveiled the rhythm of the heart. She will guide you to elevate your mindset to unprecedented heights. You are about to embark on a journey to discover your destiny through the untold narrative of Professor Jerushia.

Buckle up the seatbelt of your mind, for this expedition will plunge you into the depths of Dancing in Darkness. The profound love and the stirring of the Holy Spirit within these pages will illuminate your mind with a deeper understanding of love and adventure. Prepare to be enthralled.

Now, I sense your readiness to delve deep into this journey. Let's embark together! Read on.

I reinforce my gratitude to Professor Jerushia for her obedience to God in penning this inspirational masterpiece.

*Professor Allen Mallari, Ph.D.*

# FOREWORD II

This decades-long tale of love has finally blossomed! Professor Jerushia's timeless story is poised to capture your heart. The fragrance it exudes will refresh your senses, and her struggles and triumphs will unveil light in the darkness, showing you a path to resilience that will make you want to shout, laugh, dance, and embark on a journey to discover your destiny in Christ.

I painted the flower on the cover of this book in the Spirit to express the hope and life that one can only find by clinging to Christ. Praise the Lord for His mighty work in Professor Jerushia, who awaits your experience!

*Nina Yang Shaw*

# CONTENTS

# Dancing in *Darkness*

*A Teenage Mother's Journey of Resilience, Self-Discovery, and Love*

A TALE OF LOVE THAT TRANSCENDS TIME AND CAPTURES THE HEARTS OF ALL WHO HEAR IT...

# INTRODUCTION

Have you ever been curious about the untold tales that lie beneath the surface of hardship? Or did you ever stop to think about the untold stories concealed behind the curtain of adversity? Brace yourself for an enthralling journey as we delve into 'Dancing in Darkness: A Teenage Mother's Journey of Resilience, Self-Discovery, and Love.' It is not just a tale but also an exploration into the profound realms of love, resilience, and self-discovery, where every page unveils a hidden narrative waiting to captivate your soul.

Through the eyes of Olivette, we will travel into a world where the dance floor becomes a stage of transformation, and the garden of life conceals hidden treasures that are waiting to be unearthed.

Olivette, a teenager and a mother, finds herself at a crossroads where the weight of adolescence and motherhood collide, and the dream of something more pulls at the strings of her heart.

Venturing into the realm of the unknown—the club—amidst pulsating music and a dimly lit dance floor, she seeks an escape from her bound realities and responsibilities. The dance floor becomes her sanctuary, momentarily relieving her from the burdens that weigh her down.

But what begins as an escape becomes a transformative journey. The club becomes the catalyst for self-discovery, a reminder that even in the darkest of times, there is always a glimmer of hope. Olivette's journey is a testament to the power of resilience, the enduring quest for love, and the unyielding pursuit of self-discovery.

Her journey takes her through diverse cultures and landscapes, where love becomes a guiding force and the pursuit of self-discovery extends to others. Olivette and her love, Nazam, become beacons of hope, inspiring others to embark on their journeys of love and self-discovery.

It is a love story that defies boundaries and expectations, a resilience that overcomes adversity, and of the relentless pursuit of self-discovery. It's a reminder that in the dance of life, we can all find moments of joy, liberation, and transformation.

**Dear Reader,**

Join me as we delve into a tale of love's many dimensions to uncover the hidden treasures in the garden of life. And as we learn, alongside Olivette and Nazam, that love's journey is a dance through the darkness—a dance of resilience, self-discovery, and above all, love.

As we journey, we understand how the movement of the *leaf* signifies the Holy Spirit and His leading through the Garden. The *Club* signifies the dark times of life, serving as a springboard to better days.

The *Garden* represents life and connection with the life of Adam
and Eve as it was in the beginning. It reflects their struggles, love, and
reconnection with purpose.

Enjoy!

*"In the soft glow of a single light, shadows dance and truths emerge, setting the stage for a journey where love begins to find its voice."*

# 1

## Under the Light

Sarah was supposed to take the upcoming shift, but she was nowhere to be found. Olivette anticipated the arrival of Baylon, knowing exactly what he would say, his apologetic smile acknowledging Sarah's absence. This incident marked the third time in a week that Sarah would be arriving late, and it was just Wednesday. Olivette could not help but wonder if it was intentional on Sarah's part, but she knew better. Sarah had encountered difficulties after her car was stolen the week before, making getting to work quite challenging.

While Olivette sympathized with Sarah's predicament, she could not ignore the inconvenience it was causing her. Covering for Sarah's extra hour was an unexpected addition to her day at work: a deviation from her plans. It was not the first time she had found herself in this position. Often, the demands of responsibility compelled her to sacrifice her time and desires for the smooth operation of the restaurant.

Even though Olivette empathized with Sarah's circumstances, a persistent frustration lingered within her. The additional workload felt like an added weight to the existing heavy burden she carried. The weariness settled in deeper as she grappled with the reality of her responsibilities as a young mother, leaving her with little flexibility. Her feelings toward Baylon, the restaurant's manager, wavered between understanding and resentment. He was a kind man, but he could also be a pain in the ass, and tonight was no different. Baylon's persistent requests for extended hours tested her patience, creating a rift between her appreciation for the job and the strain it placed on her personal life. While she valued her employment as well as the sense of stability it provided, the continual demands threatened to tip the delicate balance she struggled to maintain.

There was an unspoken tension—an unyielding battle between the demands of the workplace and her yearning for a more flexible, understanding environment. As she reluctantly agreed to cover for Sarah, she felt resigned and silently hoped for empathy. It was a constant battle between the weight of her obligation and her yearning for more compassion from her employer.

The day went by with the clinking of dishes and the whirlwind of the restaurant's activities, creating a backdrop to Olivette's persistent internal struggle—a struggle familiar yet relentless.

She was fine with covering Sarah's shift if she didn't have responsibilities—responsibilities that poured upon her young head due to a mistake in the past. She had wished this week would be different from her usual routine, but did not wish for the extra hour. She did not have it in her to bear Baylon's jabs at her sluggishness. It was not her regular shift, so it was not like she could do anything about being tired. She could not wait for the night to end.

When Sarah eventually made it in, she rushed into the restaurant, flustered, apologizing for her lateness.

"I did not know you had it in you. Baylon smiled playfully at Olivette as she grabbed her coat. Baylon—she had always wondered what a weird name that was. "If you continue this way," he continued, "you are right on your way to a promotion."

*That's hard to believe!* She contributed her fair share. Not only did everyone see it, but there was also a child present. Despite the difficulty, she still managed to do it. With great effort, she smiled as wide as possible and said her goodbye to Sarah. Baylon walked her to the back of the store to close and wished her a good night.

As the sun dipped low on the horizon, casting a warm glow across the small town, the whisper of the evening breeze caressed Olivette's skin as she hurried through the cobblestone streets, the bounce in her steps a blend of determination and weariness. She was a 16-year-old mother at the crossroads of her young and tender life, her forehead etched with the weariness of the tumultuous years. She longed to be free from the shackles of past regrets. Having come a long way from where she used to be, she hoped for something new and different from her miserable life.

"I can't do this anymore," she whispered fervently, "I just can't," rubbing her exposed arms before pulling up her coat to fight against the night's cold breeze. No longer able to contain the weight of her misery, she crouched in the corner of the sparsely populated street, hugging her knees tightly and fitting her head into the nest of her arms. She yearned to cry away her fear and misery. The responsibilities, disrespect by the community, disappointment, and regret were draining and weighing her down.

Nothing, they say, prepares you for an untimely adulthood.

Why did she have to grow up so fast?

She decided to do something different that night. It was a typical night, the same as yesterday, the day before, and even two days before. After working her shift, she usually takes the 45-minute drive home. She lived with the love child's father, who was 12 years older than her 16 years tender age, residing at the edge of the town. That night, she wanted to do something different, so she made a daring decision. With a flicker of rebellion in her eyes, she resolved to go to the club. The pulsating music and dimly lit dance floor seemed to hold the promise of momentarily shedding her burdens and embracing a carefree existence. She ignored her phone ringing in her purse.

"Honey, you'll have to wait," she whispered into the night. She raised her head and stood, but felt a jolt in the air and a spring in her step. There was a shift in the air.

*How did I get here? She wondered.* "What is this?" She thought aloud as she found herself standing in the middle of an abandoned street. It was quiet and dark. The air was fresh in Las Vegas. There is no familiar smell of Madam Beatrice's bakery. An ominous feeling crept through her. The last thing she wanted was to be maimed, so what was she doing in this place? She hugged herself tightly and started walking. She turned into a corner that looked like the back alley of an abandoned warehouse. It was abandoned for sure, but it wasn't a warehouse. The building was a dilapidated, multi-story building that blocked the sky. The structure, which appeared to have once been grand, was weathered. There were shards of broken glasses, maybe bottles, and waste remains, as if a sanitation truck came and went in a hurry. When she looked up, it looked like buildings which window seals were barely clinging onto their hinges, as if surrendering to time and neglect. They looked like they would fall any minute, so she stepped away and turned to the other side. At least that explained the broken glasses. On her left, she could see a wall that was an artist's canvas bearing graffiti that whispered the tale of the impoverished, who should somehow have found solace within the decaying walls. What stood out was the heavy graffiti that read: Where Lost Souls Live.

*"Not creepy at all,"* Olivette thought with sarcasm as she felt a chill run down her spine, her heartbeat going up a few decibels. The alley carried an uncanny weight that housed secrets.

It was still, and amidst the stillness, she felt an eerie presence, like someone watching her. She heard faint rustles and whispers of echoes coming from the walls as she stood on one edge. The decrepit state of the building and the unsettling sensations it stirred within Olivette made her curious.

She decided to step back when she heard the faint plastic wrinkle, and her eyes fell on something that looked faintly like cat eyes. A typical teenager in a situation like this would be running, but Olivette was not a typical teenager, and she was not in a typical situation. Curious and moving even deeper into the dark corner, she realized it was just the glimmer of a foil paper caught in the reflection of an adjacent street light. By now, she had moved deeper into the alley, and pitch darkness surrounded her.

Following a faint whisper, she then heard running feet. A quick movement caught her attention, like a dark shadow stretching toward her. She spun, her heart pounding in her chest, but the shadowy figure dissolved into the ground, leaving her questioning whether it was a figment of her imagination. It was as if the building housed the boundary between the living and the dead.

"Oh no! Oh no, no, no." She clutched the band of her jeans and breathed through her mouth, "I am not ready to die, not like this." She said this as she trembled with fear.

"My daughter." She heard a faint voice. Fear was all over her as she looked around in panic, picking up a stick that looked like it would break if she shook it too much. "I don't even know where I am." She began thinking of all the things she wanted to do and the life she would never have if she suddenly lost her life here in this cold and dirty alley. She knew she was nowhere near home. She was lost. She retreated even deeper into the alley, using the darkness as a cover until the threat was neutralized or gone. Soon, there was silence and she sprinted out of the alley into a busy street.

"Help!"

Nobody seemed to have heard anybody scream for help from an alley. People were mostly minding their businesses. In front of her were Trice's cookies; beside them was the store where she worked and a long line of busy stores closing. Her purse fell from her hand, and she bent down to pick it up, looking at it like a foreign object. Then she remembered why she was there. And before she knew it, she was on her way to her car. She returned in the same direction she had run, and the lamp post where she crouched beside lit a bookstore. No alley. Had the alley been a mere imagination?

SOUL CITY, the city's major club, stood beside the bookstore with purple fluorescent lining the entrance, the buzz of a long queue of people and the 'boom' of the club's speakers. *Just what I need,"* she thought. "The club, not the bookstore," she said out loud, conversing with herself.

As if she had just come out of a very realistic daydream, she decided to go in, the music becoming more apparent and louder. She walked straight to the buff bodyguard by the entrance and asked to go in. The man stared at her with cold, hard eyes. She raised her head to meet his gaze and lightly touched his hands, giving him a coy smirk.

"Hey, Roy."

He was not moving. It felt like greeting a block of ice, except this one was flesh with bulks of muscle in black apparel.

"Oi, Olly. You know I can't let you in."

"Come on. Just this one time." She did a sultry left dip with her hips. "I feel so messed up. I need this." He wasn't budging. Roy was a neighbor and a regular at the restaurant who liked to talk about his experiences outside town. He had always looked out for her since that incident a year ago. She liked their conversations and craved to see the things he had seen. "Come on." She forced a streak of tears, looking at Roy with as much pain as she could show on her face, and with that, Roy's hard exterior melted.

"Just this once, Olly." His brows creased with worry, and he squeezed her shoulder. "Whatever it is, I know you'll get out of it somehow. Instead of reacting with eye-rolling and shoving, she exercised restraint. She gave him a one-sided shrug as he stepped aside for her." "Yeah. Thanks," she said, hurrying into the club before he changed his mind.

Whatever got her to this point was partly her fault, but she deserved happiness. There was no one waiting for her, anyway. There is no one to call at home. No one except her one-year-old daughter, Camile. She was alone.

She had gotten so used to balancing the weight of teenage hood and motherhood, but it had become overwhelming, and she longed to escape from the realities and responsibilities surrounding her. *How does anyone get themselves to this point of despondency?* She wished she could open her eyes and dream of a new reality, but she could not afford the luxury of daydreams or the precision of an imagined reality.

Olivette stepped into a world of vibrant energy and rhythmic beats as the heavy doors swung open. The thumping bass reverberated through her whole body, and Olivette began to nod to the heavy beats, momentarily drowning out her chaotic life. The dance floor beckoned her like a grand stage, awaiting her grand entrance.

With each step she took, the lights seemed to cascade around her like a shower of stardust. It felt like she was performing before millions, basking in the spotlight.

Whitney Houston's "I Wanna Dance with Somebody" came up, and she began a burst of energy while feeling weightless. It felt like a pump of adrenaline that she desperately needed. The music was loud, but very comforting. Song after song, she swayed left and right, swinging her arms to the melodies of the music. When Donna Summer's timeless classic, "Love to Love You Baby," began to play, she let go of her inhibitions, surrendering herself as she danced to the music. It was as if her movements were removing her pain—a testament to her strength and resilience. Men approached, eager to join her, but she gracefully declined their advances. It was her time under the lights, and she refused to share the stage with anyone else.

As the night unfolded, Olivette danced with a newfound sense of freedom. With each twirl and sway, she felt the weight of her responsibilities slowly dissipate. For this moment, the club was her sanctuary, where she could momentarily forget the challenges outside its walls. Olivette found solace under the vibrant lights and the sound of the music. In that moment, she embraced the power within herself to rise above her hardships. The dance floor became her stage, and she was the star of her show.

She did not know that this night would mark the start of an odyssey. It would be the beginning of a transformative journey. The club would become more than just an escape; it would catalyze self-discovery and be a reminder that there is always a glimmer of hope in the darkest of times. Dancing the night away and letting the lights guide her, she silently vowed to find her path, navigate the complexities of her young life, and create a future that would defy all expectations.

In this brief moment of ecstasy, she got lost under the psychedelic lights. Although she was unaware of it, she had entered a different realm. She only felt a lightness about her; as if a heavy weight were being lifted off her shoulders. She was in a world materialized by her adversities and despondent predicaments; a tear created by necessity and desperation.

As the night raced on, Olivette heard her name. Although it was a whisper, it was urgent and harsh, but she didn't care. She continued her dance, hoping whoever it was would just leave her alone. The voice came again, this time louder. She stopped momentarily, looking around to see who was calling her, but there was no one. She was still inside the club, and the atmosphere was the same. Everyone around her was dancing, some with drinks in their hands while others were vaping the night away, and no one seemed to have heard anything, so she closed her eyes against the light to resume her dance. She still had a few minutes left.

She heard her name again. As if pulled hurriedly from a haze, she opened her eyes and looked around frantically to see who the voice belonged to, but no one seemed particularly eager to talk to her. A familiar sense of dread filled her, and she remembered the alley. She grabbed her coat and hurried out of the club, stopping briefly outside to say goodbye to Roy.

She rushed to her car and jumped in quickly, shivering and holding onto the steering wheel. She hit her head lightly on her joined hands. "What is going on?" She whispered. "What do you want from me?" She screamed as she rolled up the window and was muffled.

After a few minutes, she turned on the radio. Immediately, a song came on: *'I heard the voice of Jesus say come on to me and rest.'*

"Oh my god, what do you want from me?" She screamed again, and this time it was louder. Feeling the need to clear her head and not wanting to go home. She turned off the radio and drove to a gas station. Her head was in different places when she got to the gas station. She was torn between her memory of the alley, the voice in the club, and the song from the radio. It was too much of a coincidence. She put on the radio again and waited patiently for the song to resume. It was the evening radio program that she always skipped, but she felt the need to listen to it that night. She focused on the words in the song: 'Come to me.'

She decided to call into the radio program to talk about her experience. She told the host that the voice of God was calling to her, and she wanted to heed the voice. She did not know when she began to cry. When she could no longer speak, she dropped the call and cried in her car.

Until that night, she had refused to speak of her past with anyone. She had given up on love and was sure she did not deserve happiness. She stopped attending church with her mother, and any mention of Jesus made her angry.

She looked out of her car window, assessing the familiarity of the town, its storefronts, and the judgmental glances of familiar faces that intensified her yearning for an escape. "I need a way out of this cycle," she murmured, a muted plea to the universe. "I deserve to be happy," she cried silently, staring into the night.

Remembering her little girl at home, she started the engine. It was time to go home.

"Oh, Camile, my baby. I'll be home soon," she whispered into the emptiness of her car. The thought of her giggles always lifted her spirit but weighed on her all at once. She would give anything to live like her love child, Camile, in the juvenile bliss of oblivion, but she was not so little. She was a mother, a teenage mom, and her experience had etched weariness into her forehead. She could not afford the luxury of pretense.

Camile was asleep when she got home. In the cradle of her crib, she found her. She reckoned her baby's father had stayed up to hear her drive in. Despite her desire to rouse them, she found herself entranced by the harmonious rhythm of her baby's father's respiration aligning with Camile's, resulting in her focus shifting to the tender features of her baby's face. Her innocence was so evident. Why did she have to bring her into this cruel world? She smiled at her mother's protective embrace. They didn't have conversations, but gestures like this reminded her of their relationship and what it meant to her. Her baby didn't know how to express how she felt. She always seemed tongue-tied, even with her father. Grateful tears filled her eyes as she realized she had his complete support for raising their daughter. She wouldn't know what to do otherwise.

Olivette arrived at the gourmet restaurant the next morning, preparing for the day's work. As she meticulously arranged the silverware on the tables, the movement at the door caught her eye. A woman stood near the entrance, conversing with her manager. He pointed his fingers towards my direction. The woman's eyes followed his fingers and landed on her.

Their eyes met, and the woman, with an air of purpose, began striding toward Olivette. It was as if they were frozen in time, and the clinking of cutlery faded into the background as the woman drew closer.

"Are you Olivette?" The woman's voice held a tone of familiarity that caught Olivette off guard and sent her spiraling. Olivette turned from the front of the counter to see a stranger standing before her. Her eyes captivated Olivette for a second, and she was held in a trance. Shaking away the fuzzy feeling, she smiled at the stranger.

"Yes, ma'am. What may I do for you?"

"I found you in the hotel's monthly 'Employee of the Month' newsletter."

Olivette's brows furrowed in surprise. "Oh." Confusion mingled with curiosity.

"I am Isabelle from 'Soulful Journey' radio."

*'Soulful Journey?'* Olivette assessed this strange visitor, who exuded a comforting familiarity.

Isabelle, sensing her confusion, quickly clarified. "You called into our program yesterday and sort of told us your name and where you worked." The woman explained, "I'm the host of the radio show. We received many calls after you shared your experience of hearing a voice calling your name while dancing in a club. I felt the need to visit."

The memories rushed back, overwhelming Olivette. Her emotions, held in check for so long, threatened to spill over. The woman's words, coupled with the mention of the haunting voice, shattered the fragile walls she had constructed.

"Mind if I have a moment?" Isabelle asked, her presence carrying a certain reassurance that resonated with Olivette's weary soul.

Tears welled in Olivette's eyes, and her voice quivered as she choked back the flood of emotions. "Yes?" It sounded more like a question than an answer. Isabelle smiled kindly and held Olivette's hands. It was as if she could see right through her, and Olivette was feeling raw with vulnerability—a mix of fear and a yearning for understanding.

The encounter, though unexpected, felt like an intrusion into a realm she had tried to look away from—a realm of unanswered questions and haunting experiences that had disrupted the very fabric of her existence. She was used to wishing away the divine, anything that stepped out of the ordinary, and convincing herself she was on a long journey.

As the weight of her unspoken turmoil hung in the air, Olivette braced herself for a conversation she hadn't anticipated, which seemed to be pushing her toward confronting the mysteries she had sought to evade. They settled at a nearby table, and Isabelle listened intently, her empathetic gaze offering a sanctuary for Olivette's weary heart. Her words were a gentle river that flowed over the stones of Olivette's worries, soothing and understanding.

"Your journey is extraordinary," Isabelle said, echoing Olivette's sentiments. "There's strength in vulnerability and power in your determination."

Isabelle told her of a journey she would have to embark on. "Many like you had gone on that journey, and I believe the Lord has called for you now. It is your time now to take this journey. If you are ready."

As Isabelle said her goodbyes, a newfound sense of purpose bloomed within Olivette. Her visit wasn't a random occurrence but a divine prompting—a confirmation that, despite the challenges, Olivette wasn't navigating this journey alone.

This encounter propelled Olivette forward onto a celestial path—an expedition towards uncovering her true self and delving into the enigmas of the spiritual world. This marked the beginning of the story of a young woman, a mother, and an aspiring visionary, guided by the illuminating lights as she commenced a voyage encompassing fortitudes, love, and self-realization.

"*Every step forward is a testament to love's quiet power—guiding us through the darkness and into the warmth of its embrace.*"

# 2

# *The Journey of Love Sets In*

A shift began after Isabelle's visit, leaving an indelible mark on Olivette. She went home after her shift at the restaurant to find the town now shrouded in peace and lit only by soft streetlights.

"Quite the night, huh?" Sarah, her colleague, commented as they exited the restaurant side by side.

Sarah had arranged to switch her shift, finding it more convenient to commute to the restaurant from home than from her other job. Olivette admired Sarah's resilience, growing newfound respect for her determination.

"Indeed, longer than usual," Olivette replied, her thoughts consumed by the day's unfolding events. "Did you see the woman who came by this morning?"

"Isabelle, right?" Sarah recalled.

"Yes, I called her radio show," Olivette mused aloud, almost to herself, as she changed out of her work attire.

"Why'd you call?" Sarah's curiosity piqued, etching a trace of interest on her face.

"Believe it or not, I heard a voice. It felt like it was guiding me to make that call. I just had this urge to share something," Olivette explained, the significance of her words palpable. "How did you even find out about that show?" Olivette pondered, a curious expression gracing her features.

Sarah grinned knowingly. "I'm a bit of a night owl. I catch the show occasionally. The stories people share... they're fascinating. I think I missed the episode with your story, though."

Pausing near her house, Sarah's curiosity about Olivette's story lingered. She asked, now enthralled by the story as it was developing, "Did they say anything about your voice?"

"Not directly, but Isabelle mentioned they received a similar call from someone else," Olivette replied, her gaze fixed on the nighttime scenery.

Olivette confided in Sarah, recounting her experiences and the unsettling incident in the alley, as Sarah listened attentively, showing a mix of curiosity and understanding.

"You know," Sarah began, her tone thoughtful, "sometimes life sends us signs, like whispers from a different universe. It's up to us to pay attention. We must decide whether we will follow the lead of the whispers or choose a different path."

She paused, letting the weight of her words settle in the quiet space between them.

"Olivette, you've got responsibilities; I get that. But don't let them blind you to the magic that might be right before you. Embrace the mysteries and the unexpected; they might just lead you to something extraordinary."

Her voice was full of wisdom and encouragement, urged Olivette to view the supernatural currents in her life not as distractions but as pathways to something bigger than herself. The conversation reassured Olivette and filled her with a newfound resolve to explore the uncharted territories before her.

She bid Sarah goodbye, choosing to take a long route home, allowing the evening breeze to wash over her. She wanted to be with her thoughts and reflect on what she had to do. The voices and tunes provided a backdrop to Olivette's thoughts.

When she got home, Eli was asleep while her baby's father was up watching a TV reality show. As she sat down to dinner, she allowed the conversations she engaged in with Sarah and Isabelle to envelope her. After dinner, she went to check on Camile. Upon entering the nursery, Olivette felt a palpable shift in the atmosphere. The room, bathed in the soft evening light, seemed to embrace the transformative energy in the air. Mundane details—scattered toys, the cradle where Camile slumbered peacefully—now took on a different hue.

Olivette took a moment to sit by the window, contemplating the events of the day—the encounter with Isabelle, the radio show hostess. They wove together into a narrative of transformation and a journey yet to be unveiled.

Later in her room, she lay in bed with Soulful Journey projecting from a radio by her bedside. The radio played softly in the background, with stories from Isabelle's callers about the mysteries of the ethereal realm. Olivette found herself drawn into the narratives that transcended the ordinary. They became fragments of a bigger story, and she wondered about the depth of life and the supernatural currents she had been oblivious to.

She traced the contours of her life with newfound clarity. She began to envision possibilities that she did not think existed before.

"How much have I missed?" she wondered aloud, her voice a whisper in the stillness of her room. "How many revelations have I overlooked?" She pondered, her gaze drifting into the night.

That night, as Olivette surrendered to the embrace of sleep, she had a mysterious dream—a tapestry woven with threads of the mystical and the unknown. She found herself in a landscape that mirrored both the familiar and the metaphysical. The moon hung low in the sky, casting a silvery, soft glow over a garden. Flowers of different kinds she had never seen before bloomed in harmony; their petals kissed by the soft caress of a gentle breeze. The air carried the sweet scent of blossoms, a fragrance that whispered secrets.

Olivette wandered through the garden with light and curious steps. The grass beneath her feet felt like fine silk and the garden heaved with a celestial symphony of night creatures, providing a melodic backdrop to her nocturnal journey. The moon, a silent witness to her exploration, painted the scene with hues of blue and grey, enabling an atmosphere of mystery and enchantment.

As she meandered through the garden, Olivette caught glimpses of figures in the shadows—ethereal beings whose features seemed to shift and morph every second. Their elegant movements heightened the otherworldly feel of the landscape.

In the clearing she found, the air crackled with pure energy, and the sweet fragrance of blooming flowers enveloped her like a gentle caress. A soft, melodic, soothing voice surrounded her as she stepped into the clearing.

"Olivette," a baritone voice reverberated through the clearing, its source hidden in the shadows.

She turned, searching for the speaker, but there was no visible figure. Instead, the voice seemed to emanate from the very fabric of the dream itself.

Whispers of curiosity escaped from her lips, blending into the serene atmosphere, as she inquired, "Could you please tell me who you are?"

"The voice replied, enveloped in an aura of ancient enigmas, "Though I am myself, it is not my being that is of significance."

The clearing transformed as the voice spoke. The flowers changed colors in response to the words of the speaker. Vines of radiant hues curled around unseen structures, creating an ephemeral architecture that seemed to materialize and fade with the tones of the voice.

"What is it that you most seek, Olivette?" The voice inquired, its intonation echoing through the dreamscape like a harmonious refrain.

"I want to understand the path beyond the ordinary, a journey into the mysteries that call my name," Olivette answered, her words blending with the dream's magical ambiance.

The moon overhead brightened as she spoke, casting a gentle glow on the garden. The ebb and flow of their speech created a visual symphony as shadows danced in unison with the voice.

"Your path is woven with threads of self-discovery and love," the voice whispered. As it did, a constellation of stars appeared overhead, a celestial tapestry mirroring Olivette's aspirations.

The dream unfolded with a seamless dance of words and imagery. The voice guided Olivette through the dreamscape, revealing visions of possibilities and untold stories. Although alone, she did not feel alone. There was a protective warmth that cascaded through her with every step she took. The dream garden unfolded around Olivette like a beautiful curtain, with every step she took revealing a new facet of its ethereal beauty. As the voice spoke, it guided her through the blossoming landscape.

"Do you see the petals beneath your feet, Olivette?" the voice asked.

"Yes, they're soft, like... silk," she replied, marveling at the petals that swayed with each step.

"These are the petals of grace," the voice explained. "They represent forgiveness and renewal. Every step in this garden is a step toward healing."

As she continued, the flora transformed, each flower offering a spectrum of colors that painted the air with a kaleidoscope of hues.

"These are the blooms of resilience," the voice continued. "The color and petal symbolize the strength to overcome challenges. Like these blooms, your journey is a testament to the beauty that emerges from the trials you face."

Olivette noticed gentle beings with iridescent wings flitting among the flowers.

"These are celestial companions, messengers of love and guidance," the voice revealed. "They dance on the breezes of inspiration, whispering the truths of your soul and nudging you toward the divine purpose woven into the fabric of your existence."

As Olivette walked deeper into the garden, the air was filled with a symphony of natural sounds—the rustle of leaves, the gentle hum of unseen insects, and the distant murmur of a tranquil stream.

"Listen, Olivette," the voice nudged her. "Every being in this garden exists in unity, like intertwined destinies. Nothing exists without the other. Each sound, each rustle, is a call, a response to the sweet melody of creation. In this garden, you are not alone."

Indeed, she was not alone. She stood, reveling in the warmth of the garden, as the voice went silent.

*"From the depths of the garden, a mysterious call echoes—whispering promises of healing, growth, and the blossoming of a love that defies time."*

# 3

## An Enigmatic Call from the Garden

The dreamscape painted a vivid representation of Olivette's upcoming spiritual journey. Each element, from petals to celestial companions, contributed to an intricate blending of the earthly and the divine.

*"In this garden, you are not alone," the voice resonated in her waking moment.*

*As Olivette stirred in her room, the tranquil morning greeted her. Nature's gentle intrusion interrupted her thoughts.*

*"That was strange," she murmured.*

A solitary leaf danced on a breeze and settled on her outstretched palm, its vibrant green and intricate patterns capturing her attention amid the morning calm.

Reaching out to touch it, a sudden gust of wind swept her across the floor, transporting her to what seemed like a forest. The scent of leaves and bark overwhelmed her senses, causing her to reel from the intense heat. Closing her eyes, she assumed it was another dream, yet she found herself back in her room. Frantically brushing the leaf away, she inadvertently touched it again and was thrust once more into the ground, this time onto sandy, marshy soil.

"Be ready." A man's voice echoed around her.

Squinting against the bright sunlight, she discerned a figure in the distance, partially obscured by the sun's rays. "Too bright!" she muttered, shielding her eyes, and trying to grasp her surroundings. "It's not a forest. It's a garden."

"Yes, Eden."

"Did I say that aloud? Ha ha ha."

The chuckle was loud and guttural, and it seemed like the trees shook along with it. Suddenly, it was brighter than it was before. She had to close her eyes.

She felt a sudden rush of wind and heard a crashing sound. She opened her eyes to see the miniature statues on the window strewn all over the floor. She was in her room again. She saw the leaf nested in her window seal. The leaf felt like a token from a world veiled in mystery, an offering from an unseen hand guiding her toward an uncharted path. Its presence spoke of an unseen force at play—an invitation to an expedition into realms unknown.

It was scary, but it felt strangely like hope. Her heart fluttered with intrigue and uncertainty, an unspoken call to a path that seemed to beckon her toward a transformation yet to be unraveled.

Her room, now bathed in the tranquil embrace of the morning, bore no traces of her dream or the mysterious voice that had summoned her. The voice came to her in her dream, and it called her softly to return to the garden—the essence of the dream lingering like a faded melody. She looked around her and stared at her surroundings.

It's been a long time since she took notice of her room or what it looked like. Stepping down from the bed and taking a slow stride towards her bedroom window, she took in the tranquil smell of the morning dew. She noticed the tiny little details exposed by the faint light of dawn.

In her room, nostalgia lingered, gentle reminders of the past, with each item carefully placed as more than just a decoration. She had miniature statues, gifts from long-gone vacations, and memories of days when her laughter was long, natural, and genuine. These items reminded her of the past, and they whispered tales of vacations and laughter shared with her mother. Among the hordes of miniature sculptures was a small Eiffel Tower, which was a token from their trip to Paris. It invoked memories of the shared delight of exploring a city so foreign yet so welcoming.

She had photographs on her dresser of frozen moments of joy and companionship, which portrayed the love and affection she shared with her daughter's father. Each frame told a story—hikes through serene trails, beach days with sandcastles and giggles, and the tender moments of quiet shared under a starlit sky. They were stories etched in the back of her childhood memory—memories she hoped to get rid of so she wouldn't feel the hurt of hope but which she was now beginning to remember. She remembered how the sun shone through the windows in the living room and how her mother would come to her room to wake her with a peck. Those days were gone, she reminded herself, and there was little to nothing she could do to bring them back. When her dad died, everything changed. Nothing was ever the same. She blamed herself for his death. She had gone into labor pretty early and her father was on his way to see her when he was crushed by a speeding truck. Her mother had taken extra hours at work while taking care of Camile for her. She was, of course, more experienced with caring for babies and she once said that she did not trust Olivette to look after Camile.

She was scared that her mother was right. She barely knew how to comfort Camile when she began to cry. She often got so frustrated with her that she began to cry with her. She shook the feeling and looked around her.

Her reading table, scattered with books and journals, held treasures of a different kind. The dog-eared pages of novels were her windows to other worlds, places where she sought solace and found understanding. Her journals, filled with handwritten musings chronicling her growth, desires, and moments of uncertainty and clarity, lay in a neat orderly pile.

A hair tie that she had carelessly thrown away after a long day and a heart-shaped studded ring that her father had given her were among the personal items she kept by her bedside. She also had a notepad where she scribbled her to-do lists every morning. She whispered a silent reminder of her ambitions and goals, a reassuring beacon in the whirlwind of daily life.

The mixture of these seemingly ordinary objects fueled the heartbeats of her existence. They weren't just items. They were memories woven into every inch of her room. Each piece carried the weight of cherished memories and future aspirations, pictures of her past, and a silent tribute to the love, warmth, and unspoken bond between mother and daughter that radiated within the very essence of the room.

"Olly, dear." It was her mother's voice.

"Find me." The gentle whisper came again. Olivette knew what she had to do. She remembered what Isabelle said.

The dream's whispers, the leaf's unexpected arrival, and the mysteries they bore left Olivette teetering on the threshold of a journey that promised a transformation she felt both unprepared for and undeniably drawn toward.

In that fleeting moment, something stirred within her, like a beacon of light that cascaded her being—a yearning for uncharted adventures and a thirst for a life beyond the confines of her teenage years and the responsibilities of motherhood. She felt an urge blossom within her, a call she could not ignore—a call to follow the leaf's silent invitation, a beacon toward the untold, a journey that beckoned her to unearth what lay beyond the known horizon. She knew what she had to do and was ready for it. It was what she had been waiting for: confirmation, a leading voice. And now that she had it, there was nothing more she was waiting for.

"Hey, baby." Her mother called again and Olivette woke with a start as the morning's light filtered through the parted curtains, accompanied by the sunrise's gentle hues. She sat up, shaking away the morning fogginess and holding on to the memory of the previous day, still stirring her thoughts. She hugged the edge of her bed as if in a trance, trying to place the memory of the strange events leading up to this moment.

"You don't want to be late for work." Her mother said this as she noticed Olivette struggling to rise from her bed.

With a surge of determination, Olivette rose from her bed, each movement a testament to the resolve burgeoning within her. Later, she joined her mother at the kitchen table, the scent of coffee and scrambled eggs swirling in the air.

"Morning, sweetheart," her mother said with a warm smile.

"Morning, Mom," Olivette replied, sleep still evident in her voice. She sipped the freshly brewed coffee, its warmth seeping into her stomach and awakening her senses. The touch of the leaf had left Olivette in a trance, the residue of its magic lingering in the muted corners of her mind. The message it carried—the call to embark on a journey—echoed in her thoughts, casting a reflective veil over the usual morning routine.

Her mother was looking at her with quiet understanding. "Did you sleep well?" she inquired, her eyes reflecting a blend of concern and maternal warmth.

Olivette nodded, a faint smile playing on her lips.

"Yes, mum." Then, after a brief silence, "mum."

"Yes, dear," her mother answered, planting a kiss on her cheek.

She forced a smile. *'How do I tell her about the dreams and the visions?'*

She shook her head slightly, confused and determined. "I... had a dream. A leaf. It told me I needed to go somewhere and do something. It's like a calling, Mom," she confessed, the words treading the delicate line between revelation and uncertainty.

Her mother paused with a strange look on her face. Olivette wasn't sure if she wanted to burst into tears and scream at her. Her mother was no stranger to life's unexpected turns, and she knew that a day like this would come. "A calling, you say?" She heaved a sigh and looked her daughter straight in the eyes. "Sometimes, life gives us signs we can't fully grasp at first, May be it is leading you to something important." "I always knew a day like this would come," her mother confessed, her gaze drifting to a place beyond the kitchen table as if glimpsing the threads of time woven into their lives. "Your father had a similar experience when he was younger, you know."

"Dad did?" Olivette gasped.

"Yes, dear. A call, a whisper from something beyond the ordinary."

Olivette's eyes widened; the mention of her father infused a feeling of longing, and she thought of the many times he would have been there to guide her. Even now, she wished he were there. Having learnt that he had a similar encounter. There would have been lots for him to say.

Her mother nodded, a small smile playing on her lips. "Yes, long before you were born. He used to talk about it—a leaf that changed the course of his life. It led him to places he never imagined and shaped the man he became. Sometimes, life nudges us toward the unknown, and we must decide whether to answer that call."

Her mother continued, "Your father embraced the adventure, and it brought him joy, challenges, and many experiences. It was his journey, just as this is yours." Just then, Camile, Olivette's one-year-old daughter woke, the soft sound echoing through the room. Olivette turned towards the source of the coos, a mixture of emotions playing on her face. "Speaking of adventures, here's my little adventurer," she said with a soft smile, lifting Camile from her crib and settling her in a highchair.

Her mother's eyes twinkled at the sight of the infant, silently acknowledging their uncanny likeness. "A budding explorer, just like her mother," she remarked, a hint of nostalgia in her tone. As they finished the rest of their breakfast, Olivette shared the details of her mysterious visions outside the restaurant while her mother absorbed the revelation. Camile observed the exchange from her highchair with wide light blue eyes and innocent curiosity.

"I'll tell your aunt May. You'll stay with her for a few days. Somehow, she understands better than anyone what this journey is really about." Her mother removed a strand of hair from her face. "You know she worried about you when you said you weren't returning to school?"

"Oh," Olivette said.

"Yes," Her mother stood at the table, the used dishes in her hand. "She was so happy when your dad decided to go on this same journey, and I believe she'll be elated to find out that you've been called too. I'll call her to let her know. She'll be so happy."

Olivette smiled sheepishly. She was overwhelmed by the level of support her mother was showing, and even more was her Aunt May, whom she hadn't seen since her dad died. "Thanks, Mum, I love you." She embraced her mother tightly, taking in her scent. Her mother hugged her back, whispering a prayer in her ears. She could feel the tremble in her voice. They were tears of joy.

"I'm so proud of you, dear." She said as she held her at arm's length. "Errm. Work."

"Oh yes."

Olivette hurried to work, sure that the rest of the day was settled. She didn't have the weight that she carried the previous day. Even Baylon noticed Olivette worked with more enthusiasm than she had ever done.

"Olivette Ridley, you seem different today. Something I should know?"

Olivette sprung her head in his direction and replied with a smile. She planned to tell him later when her shift ended, but it was just an hour away, so she decided to have a private moment with him.

"Actually, yes. Can I talk to you at the back?"

"Is everything okay?" Baylon's tone had shifted from shared excitement to worry. She knew what her absence would mean. There weren't very many hands at the restaurant, and her leaving would pour the brunt of the work on him. She wished she had a choice, but she had no intention of changing her mind. So, she relays her intention as crispy as possible.

Confusion was all over his face, and he asked her, "Did something happen?"

"No." She smiled kindly.

"Is it about the woman who came here yesterday? Did she come to recruit you?"

"What? No." Olivette knew he was simply grasping the most logical explanation, but she didn't have much time. "I wanted to wait until my shift was over, but you asked, and I decided to tell you."

She spent the rest of the evening serving customer after customer as briskly as possible. It was as if she had taken extra care of her customers.

Back home, in her room, she embraced herself as all her childhood memories came washing over her. She packed a small bag, knowing deep within that this was her chance to peel back the layers of her identity, reveal hidden truths, and explore the depths of her uncharted potential.

The garden was the sanctuary she had been looking for. It held the promise of growth, transformation, and the allure of love—a canvas upon which her journey of self-discovery and understanding would unfold. She would start from the known to the unknown, keeping her mind open to the divine voice guiding her path. It was a pilgrimage toward the core of her being, a quest to comprehend the whispers of her soul and to unfold the chapters of her story that were yet to be written.

She wasn't sure how long it would be. She was however willing to trust the voice. With different items carefully nestled in her bag, Olivette felt a sense of burgeoning excitement, a newfound resolve to embark on an odyssey that promised more than just exploration—it offered the potential for self-realization and the discovery of an existence beyond the confines of the known.

Ready to step into the unknown, Olivette's heart beat with the rhythm of anticipation, echoing the tale of a transformative journey set to unfold.

She couldn't help but feel a deep sense of gratitude towards her mother, who had always showered her with love, especially during this trying time. The time had come for her to start this journey, not just for herself but also for the sake of her child. She hoped to be a better person in her pursuit. By pursuing her happiness, she would become a better mother and a role model for her daughter.

She found the leaf just where it had been in the trance, wedged in her window. When she touched it, she felt a force of electricity weave through her as she felt a lightness take over her limbs. She gasped as her legs threatened to give way. Finding her balance, she placed the leaf within the pages of her Bible. She felt the presence of the words settle over her as she placed the holy book in her duffel, which she later switched for a backpack.

She would set out into the world under the leaf's enigmatic presence, listen to its whispers, and follow her intuition. The path ahead was unknown, but she was filled with a newfound sense of purpose and a belief that love would guide her steps. With each passing moment, Olivette felt herself shedding the weight of her past and embracing the possibilities of her future. The journey of love had begun, and she was determined to follow it wherever it led.

As night fell and the stars began to sparkle, Olivette felt ready to embrace the unknown. Despite knowing the journey ahead wouldn't be easy, she felt equipped with the strength and resilience she discovered during her teenage years and motherhood.

With the leaf as her guide and love as her compass, Olivette was prepared to venture into self-discovery and pursue the mysterious garden. She understood the forthcoming journey would challenge her in ways she couldn't foresee, but her determination to carve her path and shape her future remained unwavering.

Drifting into sleep, Olivette made a silent vow to herself: to welcome the journey, nurture the love within, and flourish like a blossoming flower in life's garden.

"Olivette," a familiar voice called out to her in the quiet of the night. It no longer frightened her; instead, it felt like a comforting presence. She smiled in response, finding solace in its familiarity, and peacefully returned to sleep, anticipating the promise of a new day ahead.

# 4

## The Call of Friendship

 Olivette woke abruptly, her heart racing from the voice that echoed in her dream, urging her to wake up and continue her journey. Despite the ethereal encounter, her room remained quiet and empty. She realized the voice was a yearning within her for something beyond the ordinary.

The morning unfolded quietly as Olivette prepared for the day ahead. Each task held a special significance, marking her imminent departure from Las Vegas. Spending time with Camile, she sang her lullabies and danced around the house.

In front of her mirror, wearing a peach t-shirt with a large flower, Olivette packed her essentials into her backpack—clothes, a notebook, a photo of Camile, and the Bible with the vibrant leaf. Today was her last day in Las Vegas, prompting farewells to her friend, Elite. Glancing at the familiar streets, she absorbed the lights, sounds, and memories, preparing to say her goodbyes.

Dialing Elite's number, Olivette shared her departure news, prompting concern from her friend. Elite was surprised and worried about Olivette's sudden decision to leave. The conversation unfolded against the backdrop of city sounds, with Olivette trying to explain her unexplained longing for something beyond the horizon.

Elite, supportive yet concerned, encouraged Olivette but requested that she stay in touch. As they exchanged their last words, the call marked for both of them an end and a beginning.

After she ended the call, Olivette felt a mix of emotions but also a surge of courage, knowing this journey was an opportunity for growth and self-discovery.

Making silent promises to herself, she bid farewell to Camile and her mother, assuring them of her return. Stepping out into the night, the city, usually bustling with life, now felt different—shadows and whispers dominating the landscape.

 Olivette embarked on her journey, feeling attuned to the universe's whispers guiding her steps. Determined to uncover the truth in the garden, she embraced the path set before her.

Venturing into the night, Olivette pondered on what lays ahead. She wondered if she'd find love or a deeper connection with herself and the world. Love was her compass as she followed the leaf's whispers, realizing that this journey held countless possibilities.

With each passing moment, Olivette felt herself growing stronger, her spirit unfurling like a blossom in the garden of life. She had answered the call, and it was time to surrender to the journey, to let love lead her to the place where her heart truly belonged.

"I am doing the right thing," she affirmed, the words carrying a weight of certainty. Once an enigmatic messenger, the leaf now symbolized courage and the embrace of the unknown. The thought of her father, who had also embarked on this journey, became a beacon of inspiration, lighting the path ahead. Camile's laughter, etched in her memory, became a source of strength—a reminder that her choice was not just for herself but for the blossoming adventure that awaited them both.

As she walked through the familiar scene of the city, she thought about her past. Olivette's journey took an unforeseen turn when she became pregnant. Her dreams of a life beyond the small town and the high school walls transformed into a reality that demanded much more than she had envisioned.

The news of her pregnancy produced a whirlwind of emotions. As the whispers of her situation circulated through the hallways, she had to deal with judgment from her peers and snide remarks from her teachers. Judgmental glances and comments painted the canvas of her teenage existence.

All these—the weight of societal expectations and the harsh reality of being a pregnant teenager—made Olivette drop out of school, a decision that wrenched her heart and sent her spiraling out of control. The once-vibrant and cheerful Olivette had become a shadow of her old self.

The impending responsibilities of motherhood cast a shadow over the dreams that had once fueled her spirit.

Once a canvas of youthful hopes, the small town reflected unfulfilled aspirations and the harsh judgments that accompanied teenage parenthood. Misery became a constant companion during those months.

The isolation from her peers, the judgmental glances, and the internal struggles for identity and self-worth wore on Olivette's spirit. The stark realities of motherhood started to replace the dreams she had woven with Benny, the child's father.

The last straw, a tragic turning point for Olivette, was when her father, on his way to be with her during her early labor, met with a fatal accident. The news crushed Olivette, with grief and guilt settling on her young shoulders. Her journey into motherhood, which was already tainted with isolation, now carried the additional burden of loss.

The small town, now a backdrop to the intertwined threads of joy and sorrow, was a witness to Olivette's story. The dreams of a blissful future that she once dreamed collided with the harshness of reality, creating a story of resilience, sacrifice, and the unforgiving nature of circumstances.

And now, as Olivette ventured into the night, the weight of her past hung heavily in the air. The decision to follow the call of the leaf was not just a quest for self-discovery but a journey toward healing, redemption, and the pursuit of a future where the whispers of hope would replace the echoes of misery.

It was time for her to let go of her past and face her future. She was done letting her past ruin her life or inscribe the hard lines of misery within her spirit.

*"With each new chapter, the journey unfolds—revealing that the path to love is as unpredictable as it is beautiful."*

# 5

# A Novel Journey Sets In

"It's going to be a big journey," Olivette said with a smile, feeling excited about starting something new.

With the determination of a kid trying a new video game, she headed to Aunt May's place, taking the bus. She felt excited but unsure of what lay ahead of her.

The city was busy with people and noise when she reached the crowded bus station. There were lots of different people doing different things. Olivette put her earphones on but kept the volume low so she could still hear what was happening around her.

The station was full of life. Some people were laughing and reading together, others were busy on their phones, and some were walking quickly. Signs showed where the buses were going and a screen told us when they'd leave.

Everyone seemed to be in a hurry or excited. While some were sitting and looking at their phones or books, others were walking back and forth. The floors and benches looked old and worn out, and you could smell coffee from a nearby shop.

There were announcements on the loudspeaker and music from a person playing a guitar. A mom was struggling with her baby's things while the baby tried to run away. That reminded Olivette of Camile. She wished she could have been more of a mother to her, but she let her resentment towards herself erode guilt in her. She always dreamed of being a mother one day, to share all the love that was waiting to pour into one who is worthy to receive such pure love. Camile, her love child, deserved of the greatest gift of love.

All she did was love and invest in all the gifts and knowledge she acquired from her life. Perhaps she was scared she would fail her, as she had failed herself. However, she remembered her last conversation with her mom and felt her heartbeat with eagerness to return home. She could feel a flutter of hope in those last moments. She hung her head back and leaned onto the bench, taking off her earphones to truly be present.

She saw people walk briskly towards arriving buses, friends reuniting with hugs and laughter, their joy echoing through the station like a contagious rhythm.

The minutes ticked away as Olivette waited, her gaze washing continuously over the eclectic crowd. While she pondered, a family walked towards the bench beside her—a young mother with an elderly couple trying to soothe a fussy baby, mimicking baby coos, came to sit by her. After the baby grew quiet, they sat quietly. She thought about how lucky they must be to be together like that, with not a hint of their troubles, which she was sure they had. Everyone had some trouble they were dealing with. The family did not seem in a hurry to leave, and she decided they were waiting for the same bus as her.

As the remaining waiting time ticked away, Olivette closed her eyes to pray for guidance and protection along the way. She kept track of the time with a clock on the station wall that marked the passage of time, its hands ticking steadily toward the scheduled departure. Soon, the distant rumble of an arriving bus resonated through the station, signaling their departure. Passengers gathered their belongings, forming a line that mirrored the diversity of their destinations. Olivette, too, rose from her bench, carrying with her the anticipation of the odyssey ahead.

As she stepped onto the awaiting bus, the station, a transient crossroads of journeys, faded into the background.

Olivette spotted an empty spot on a bench beside a young woman engrossed in a book. It was the woman soothing the baby.

"Excuse me, is this seat taken?" Olivette inquired with a friendly smile.

The woman looked up, her eyes momentarily leaving the pages. "Oh, no, go ahead! Plenty of room."

Seated, Olivette adjusted the strap of her bag and struck up a conversation. "Heading somewhere exciting?"

The woman grinned. "Just a little weekend getaway. Sometimes you need a break, you know?"

"Absolutely. Where to?"

"A quaint little town upstate. I just need a change of scenery. What about you?"

"Visiting my aunt May. It's been a while."

"Family time is the best time," the woman said, closing her book. "By the way, I love your bag. Is that leather?"

"Yeah, a gift from my dad. He had a thing for well-made things."

"That's sweet. I'm Emma, by the way."

"Olivette. Nice to meet you, Emma."

While they waited for the bus to move, the two women exchanged stories, dreams, and the random adventures that had brought them to this shared moment. Although Olivette wasn't usually one to talk, she allowed their conversation to grow. Emma was a good talker, so it was easy to converse with her. The lively banter continued, transforming the wait for the bus into a transient but memorable chapter in the larger narrative of their journeys.

As Olivette eased into the bench, the hum of the bus leaving the station provided a comforting cadence to their budding conversation.

"So, Olivette, what leads you to your Aunt May's?" Emma asked out of genuine curiosity, her eyes sparkling with interest.

"Life, you know. It takes unexpected turns. But I thought it was time for a visit," Olivette replied, a subtle smile playing on her lips.

"Life, huh? The ultimate plot twists. Tell me more," Emma leaned in, her expression a canvas of eagerness.

Olivette chuckled. "Well, there's a lot to unpack. I'm a single mom working to make ends meet. But I've got this little spark of wanderlust that won't fade."

"Single mom? How old are you?"

"Sixteen," Olivette replied, turning red.

"Wow. A superhero in disguise," Emma remarked, her admiration evident.

Olivette turned to face her, not sure if she was pulling her legs. She was used to people judging her. No one had ever sounded remotely impressed with her being a single mom as a teenager. She was used to the "oh" and "eh" that quickly filled their mouths.

"Well, a sleep-deprived one," she chuckled, stroking her arms nervously. "What about you? What's your story?" Olivette asked, genuinely curious.

Emma leaned back, her eyes distant momentarily, before she began, "Oh, the classic. Corporate drone by day and a dreamer by night. Hence, the spontaneous weekend getaway."

Intrigued, Olivette encouraged her to share more. "Corporate drone? Is it that bad?"

"Oh, yes. A hell of a lot of work."

"Tell me about it."

Emma sighed, "Picture this: a cubicle with a view of the water cooler, endless meetings, and the continuous whirring of an office printer."

The animated way she described it made it easy to imagine. Olivette could picture it. She compared it to the trudge of eaters at her restaurant job.

"Must be something," Olivette said, acknowledging how much a routine could become quite a hassle.

"Yep. That's my world, from nine to five. But in the muted hours of the night, I escape into the world of possibilities. That's where the real magic happens."

Olivette found herself drawn into Emma's narrative, a tale of navigating the corporate world while harboring dreams that transcended the confines of the office walls. *There's a resilience in her, a dedication to her dreams despite the monotony of corporate life. It's like she's dancing on the edge of a balance beam, and I can't help but admire her grace.'*

Olivette, deeply engrossed in Emma's stories of corporate life and dreams, couldn't resist delving deeper into the symphony of Emma's experiences. Emma shared stories of midnight musings, of projects that fueled her passion, and of the relentless pursuit of a work-life balance that often felt elusive.

Olivette leaned forward, her eyes reflecting curiosity. "Your world sounds both challenging and fascinating. How do you find the balance between that and your dreams?"

Emma smirked: her gaze thoughtful. "Ah, the eternal struggle. I try to infuse a bit of my dreams into the corporate grind. It's about finding joy in the little victories, like turning a mundane report into a piece of art."

Olivette contemplated Emma's words. Infusing dreams into every day. *Can I do the same with my responsibilities?*

Olivette continued to ask questions in response to Emma's wisdom.

"What about moments when the pursuits become overwhelming?"

Emma paused: her expression thoughtful. "Honestly, I have my moments. But then, I remind myself of the bigger picture. Every project, every late night, is a step closer to my dreams. It's about seeing the marathon beyond the sprint."

Olivette considered Emma's perspective. A marathon is beyond the sprint. *"Maybe my journey is a marathon too,"* she thought.

Olivette, with a hint of vulnerability, shared her thoughts. "What about moments of self-doubt? I sometimes feel like I'm navigating uncharted waters."

Emma nodded knowingly. "Ah, self-doubt, the uninvited companion. I remind myself that it's okay not to have all the answers. Embracing the unknown can lead to the most beautiful discoveries."

Olivette considered Emma's perspective. *'Embracing the unknown. Perhaps that's the key to unraveling my journey.'*

As Emma shared her experiences, Olivette found not only a friend on the bus but also a guide whose insights would accompany her on the odyssey ahead. She was sure this encounter was not by chance. In whatever way, this conversation will serve a purpose in the future. They weaved their way through the intricacies of her life, ambition, and the pursuit of dreams.

Olivette gazed at the passing scenes—the city's heartbeat pulsed through the crowded streets, each person a protagonist in their own story. As the bus trundled, Olivette listened to snippets of conversations—a medley of lives intersecting briefly before diverging again. The bus made intermittent stops, welcoming new passengers who brought with them their own stories and destinations. Olivette, a silent observer of the urban panorama, pondered the interconnectedness of lives within the bustling city.

Olivette found solace in the anonymity of the journey. The bus ride gave her time and space to reflect, carrying her through the threshold of her past toward the unknown horizons of her future.

Between changing landscapes and the regular hum of the bus, memories of Olivette's father surfaced in her mind like a gentle tide. She could almost hear his laughter, the way it would ring through the house when she told him a silly joke. She recalled the warmth of his encouragement when she struggled with a course at school. When he died, she could not imagine herself going back to school. After all, it was her fault that he died, fixing a problem she created. In the soft lull of the journey, she recalled the values he instilled—resilience, kindness, and an unwavering sense of responsibility.

He always used to have the right words. On one of their quiet evenings, they sat on the porch, the world bathed in the hues of the setting sun.

"Dad, do you ever worry about the future?" she'd asked.

He had responded with a gentle smile, saying, "Worrying won't change a thing, sweetheart. But preparing and living fully—that's within our control."

Olivette closed her eyes to the memory: His wisdom was always comforting. *I wish you were here, Dad.'* He always used to wrap his hands around her like a protective cloak. Little did she know how crucial his words would become. As her mind drifted further, a shadow of guilt cast itself over her thoughts, a weight she had carried since the day her father rushed to be by her side.

That dreadful night—the phone call, the urgency in his voice. She was in labor, and he was on his way to the hospital. The guilt, like a silent specter, haunted her. If only she hadn't been a reason for him to be on that road.

The weight of responsibility and guilt intertwined, creating a complex surge of emotions within her.

She whispered to herself, *"I should have known he'd drive through anything to be there. Maybe I wouldn't have called him."* The memory of that night was a wound that refused to fully heal and a constant reminder of a moment that altered the course of her life.

She remembered the promise she had made to herself—a promise to embark on this odyssey not merely for personal discovery but as a pilgrimage toward becoming a better person. With each passing mile, the city outside and the memories within merged into a mosaic of reflection.

She envisioned her daughter, Camile, and her mother as pillars of her world. She held the promise she made to them close to her heart, like a sacred oath. Camille's innocent laughter and her mother's unwavering support became guiding lights for her journey.

*"I will return,"* Olivette whispered to herself, a vow carried by the bus's gentle vibrations. *"I will return as a better person, for Camile, for my mother, for my community."* The echoes of her commitment

lingered in the air, a silent anthem underscoring the significance of her quest.

The promise she made to herself, sealed within the cocoon of the bus' journey, became a guiding beacon. With her father's spirit as a silent companion, Olivette embraced the unfolding chapters of her odyssey, determined to return as a beacon of light and inspiration for those she held dear.

As the bus approached Aunt May's neighborhood, Olivette wondered what impending mysteries awaited her. The bus ride was a brief interlude in the grand narrative of her journey, serving as a prelude to the transformative chapters that lay ahead.

At Olivette's stop, Aunt May, a kind and slender woman in her mid-forties, stood by her pickup truck, her eyes lit with anticipation. Her warm smile exuded genuine excitement while waiting for Olivette at the bus station. Her slim frame carried an air of grace, and her features reflected her wisdom and kindness.

When Olivette's mother spoke of her, it was always with a smile, because she did not carry her burdens with her. She was a beacon of light for people around here. Olivette wanted to know where she got the light in her eyes from. Since she had known Aunt May, she had never seen her frown. Even when her father died, she provided a soothing voice for everyone. She recalled the scene like a not-too-far memory.

Aunt May's eyes carried the fine lines of her year, sparkling with a warmth that put those around her at ease. Her chestnut hair, neatly pulled back into a ponytail, hinted at her practical yet caring nature. Dressed in a comfortable pair of jeans and a loose-fitting floral blouse, her charm matched her welcoming demeanor. Leaning against her pickup truck, she had the energy of someone ready to embrace both the ordinary and the extraordinary. The truck had served her for so many years and journeyed with her through many towns and state lines. It was her sturdy companion. The truck also showed Aunt May was a practical woman and reliable too. Aunt May had had this truck for so many years that she could not imagine being without it.

Olivette smiled at the 'Déjà vu' of the moment. Aunt May's smile widened, and she waved. Her eyes filled with genuine joy as Olivette stepped out of the bus.

"Olivette, honey, it's so good to see you!" They shared a warm embrace and Olivette remembered how much she missed it.

"Aunt May, it feels like it's been forever. Thank you for picking me up."

Placing a hand on Olivette's shoulder, she said, "Nonsense, dear. The family looks out for each other. Now, hop in! We've got a brief journey ahead." She went to her side of the truck and watched Olivette go around to the other side. "I see you packed light."

"Yes. I don't need much where I am going."

Aunt May nodded her approval, allowing Olivette to get into the truck before she started the engine.

As Olivette climbed into the pickup truck, the worn but well-maintained interior told stories of the countless adventures Aunt May had undertaken. The engine purred to life, a familiar melody.

Aunt May glanced at Olivette. "So, spill the beans, my girl. What is this about a pilgrimage? Your mom said something about a journey."

Olivette, taking a deep breath, replied, "It's a bit complicated, Aunt May. I just felt this calling, you know? Like there's something out there waiting for me."

"Sometimes, life throws curveballs, and we just have to swing," Aunt May replied, nodding in agreement with Olivette's confession. "I've seen my share of unexpected turns. Tell me more."

Looking out the window, Olivette gathered her words: "I had this dream, and it felt like a message. Like, there's a path I need to follow for myself and Camile."

"Dreams have a funny way of pointing us in the right direction. Your father used to say that but what does your heart say, dear?"

"It says I need to find something—something more. And maybe, in the process, I'll discover parts of myself I never knew existed." Olivette rubbed the middle of her chest lightly.

"Well, then, you're in for an adventure, aren't you? Your mom will be thrilled that you're here, even if it's just for a while."

As the pickup truck ambled along the winding roads, Aunt May cast a thoughtful glance at Olivette. The soft hum of the engine accompanied her words, weaving a tale of resilience and redemption.

"Your dad, God rest his soul, was a remarkable man. Did your mom ever tell you about the time he finished college?"

Olivette shifted, curious now that she had mentioned her dad. "Not really. Mom always kept those stories close to her heart."

Not surprised that was the case, Aunt May nodded, understanding, "Your dad had his share of struggles, sweetheart. Fresh out of college, he found himself entangled in a web of drugs. It was a dark time for him, and he felt lost."

"I never knew..."

Without missing a beat and picking her words carefully, she continued, "But, you see, even in the darkest of times, there's a glimmer of light. Your dad felt a calling, much like the one you're feeling now. It was a pull towards rehabilitation, towards rediscovering himself."

As Aunt May spoke, the landscape outside seemed to echo the tale of her father's journey—a journey that ultimately led him to a path of redemption.

"Your dad went on this soul-searching journey, determined to break free from the chains that held him down. It wasn't easy, but he found strength he didn't know he had."

"And Mom?"

Aunt May smiled and said, "Ah, your mom was a beacon of hope for him. They met during his rehabilitation journey. Love has this magical way of healing, you know?"

Olivette whispered, "I had no idea... I always thought they met like normal people—in a church, a mall, or at a restaurant—and fell in love."

Aunt May's laughter rang through the truck as she shook her head. "Life has a way of surprising us. Your dad's journey not only transformed him but also led him to the love of his life. And here you are, a testament to that love."

As Aunt May shared this chapter of Olivette's father's life, the weight of the past and the promise of new beginnings hung in the air. As she pulled up into the driveway of her house, Aunt May turned to Olivette with a reassuring smile, her eyes reflecting both warmth and determination.

"Sweetheart, I want you to know that you've got a support system here. I'll help whichever way I can, every step of the way, until you're ready to embark on your journey."

"Aunt May, I can't thank you enough. I didn't expect this, and I feel so blessed to have you by my side."

"Oh dear, it's nothing," Aunt May retracted, slapping Olivette's hand lightly. "Family looks out for one another. Your dad, God rest his soul, would have wanted the same. We'll figure this out together, okay?"

"Okay. I just... I need to do this. for Camile and me. I feel like there's something out there waiting for me."

"And you're going to find it, my dear. Sometimes, life takes us on unexpected journeys, and we discover things we never knew we were looking for."

Aunt May's support and assurance made Olivette feel comforted, helping her look ahead to the future without the fear that had troubled her before.

*"In the rhythm of resilience, we find the strength to rise, to move forward, and to dance even in the face of life's greatest trials."*

# 6

# The Dance of Resilience

"Aunt May, it's been a week, and I haven't heard anything. No whispers, no guidance. I'm starting to worry if I made the right decision."

In Aunt May's home, Olivette wrestled with the silence that had suddenly enveloped her dreams since she arrived. She became anxious in the guiding's absence voice. She was with Aunt May in the living room. The flames in the fireplace flickered as a warm backdrop to their conversation.

Aunt May touched Olivette's shoulder, nudging her closer. "Sweetheart, sometimes the universe has its timing. You've taken a step towards the unknown, and it's perfectly natural to feel lost in the silence. But remember, just because you can't hear doesn't mean it's not there."

"I just thought... I thought this journey would be clearer and that the signs would be more evident. What if I'm making a mistake?"

"Oh, my dear, uncertainty is a part of every journey. Your daddy used to say, 'The destination may be unclear, but it's the journey that shapes us.' Trust in the process, Olivette. Sometimes, the answers come when we least expect them."

The crackling of the fire seemed to echo Aunt May's words, each pop plastering the essence of her words into Olivette's mind. She had to believe what Aunt May was saying, otherwise, she would lose her faith and fervor.

"I just think whatever I do now will affect Camile's future. I don't want her to have to suffer because of me. What if I can't provide the stability she needs?"

When Camile was a newborn, she contemplated giving her away. She remembered it was Aunt May who talked her out of it. She was a raging fire, threatening to burst. So many things had gone wrong for her at the same time during that period. Because the father of her daughter had denied having anything to do with her, people were quick to call her a prostitute, an irresponsible girl. When she kept Camile, she caught glimpses of older mothers whispering under their breaths when she went out with her. She stopped going out with her because of this.

When she stopped, another round of rumors arose. Some speculated that she had killed the baby. The rumor didn't end until her mother made a show of it by taking Camile everywhere with her. She decided school wouldn't be good for her. She didn't want to answer the question that she knew would come. When the new school year started, she did not resume, much to the chagrin of her mother. Instead, she took a job. Of course, people had a lot to say about it, but it was easier to ignore them while taking orders and serving strangers.

Aunt May, understanding, assured her, "You're doing your best for Camile, and that's what matters. Life doesn't come with guarantees, but your love and commitment shine through. As for the guidance you seek, perhaps it's just taking a moment to let you find your way."

"I just wish I had a sign, something to tell me I'm on the right path."

"Give it time, dear. Signs have a way of appearing when we least expect them. And remember, you're not alone in this. You have family, friends, and the love of your little one."

The uncertainty lingered, but Aunt May's words provided a soothing antidote for her fears. There was a quiet reassurance that, in time, the whispers of guidance would find their way back to her.

The next morning, the rhythm of livestock on Aunt May's farm gave Olivette purpose. The morning sun cast a golden hue over the landscape as Olivette immersed herself in the daily tasks with the animals. With their playful bleats, the goats roamed the fenced pasture, and other livestock grazed contentedly under the watchful gaze of the farmhouse.

Armed with a bucket of feed, Olivette approached the goat pen. Their curious eyes met hers, and she couldn't help but smile at their endearing antics. As she dispersed the feed, the goats gathered around, creating a lively tableau of farm life.

"You've got the touch with those goats." Aunt May's voice called from her porch, "They seem to like you."

Olivette grinned. "I guess we've formed a mutual agreement not to give me a hard time. They are adorable."

The farm life was a therapeutic respite for Olivette. Tending to the animals, mucking out the stables, and embracing the simplicity of rural chores allowed her mind to find a momentary escape from the complexities of her journey.

Aunt May joined Olivette on the farm. "There's a kind of peace in farm life, isn't there? Each task connects us to the earth and its cycles."

Olivette nodded in agreement. "It's grounding. I find solace in the ambiance. The simplicity projects a beauty that one only finds in places like this."

As the day unfolded, Olivette's hands, once accustomed to the concrete jungles of the city, adapted to the tactile dance of rural chores. Each interaction with the farm animals echoed a timeless connection between humans and the earth. Amidst the sounds of bleating goats and the rustle of wind through the fields, Olivette found a temporary haven—a place where the whispers of guidance could blend harmoniously with the serenity of rural life.

That night, Olivette dreamt again. This time, the voice came to her as a gentle murmur.

*"Olivette, seeker of the unseen, watch as fate weaves your path."*

*In the dream, Olivette's surroundings shimmered with an otherworldly glow, and a pathway of soft light beckoned her forward. Each step was guided as if the very ground beneath her feet moved and nudged her movements, resonating with a purpose known only to the universe.*

*"I've been waiting, wondering, and seeking guidance. Are you here to show me the way?"*

*"The journey is both the destination and the revelation, young one. Embrace the unknown, for within it lies the essence of your transformation."*

*As the voice spoke, constellations danced in the night sky, and the dream changed its face. In her dreamscape, time and space seemed to intertwine, where the ordinary boundaries of reality gave way to the extraordinary.*

*"What must I do? Where does this path lead?"*

*"Your heart carries the compass, and your spirit carries the map. Trust in the whispers of the wind, the rustle of leaves, and the beating of your own heart. The answers you seek are woven into the fabric of your existence."*

*The voice revealed that she would face several challenges along the way, none of which they didn't think she could overcome. "The challenges will test your resilience and your desire to be transformed."*

With those words, the scenery shifted, revealing glimpses of the journey ahead. She saw the challenges she would encounter, her heart skipping at each revelation.

As the dream faded, the voice lingered, leaving Olivette with a sense of purpose that transcended the boundaries of the dream realm. She woke up with a new sense of purpose. Aware of the challenges she would face, Olivette pondered the entire day, praying fervently that she was strong enough to carry on.

The next day, she bade her aunt goodbye and set out on her way, ready for the challenges she would encounter. As Olivette stepped away from the comforting embrace of Aunt May's farm, her first challenge began—the unpredictable dance with transportation.

She had traveled a distance between Aunt May's farm and the garden and the narrow country road stretched before her, winding through fields and disappearing into the horizon. With her little bag cradled on her shoulder, Olivette felt the weight of the journey settling on her.

The voice had told her, "During these challenges, you will uncover the strength within you that transcends the ethereal. Life's struggles are the threads that weave the fabric of your transformation. Embrace each obstacle, for they are the stepping stones toward the garden that awaits you."

The road seemed longer than she remembered. Each step echoed the uncertainty of what lay ahead. She glanced at the sporadic passing cars, hopeful for a benevolent soul willing to offer a ride. But the road remained eerily quiet as if the universe had pressed pause on the flow of vehicles.

The heat intensified as the sun climbed higher in the sky, casting a shimmering mirage over the asphalt. Beads of sweat formed on Olivette's forehead as beads of worry began forming in her mind. The struggle to secure transportation became not just a physical hurdle but a reflection of the broader challenges she faced on this odyssey.

She extended her arm, thumb outstretched, yet the passing cars seemed oblivious to her silent plea. Doubt crept in and a knot tightened in her stomach. Why did it feel like the world had turned a blind eye to her journey?

Once a symbol of possibility, the road stretched ahead like a daunting path. Each failed attempt at securing a ride chipped away at Olivette's resolve. She clutched her bag a little tighter as if shielding her from the weight of the challenges that were already pressing against her shoulders.

Doubt intertwined with determination in Olivette's thoughts. The hum of passing cars became a reminder of the rhythm of the life she struggled to rejoin. In these moments of rejection, her mind oscillated between questioning her decision to embark on this journey and affirming the necessity of reaching the elusive garden.

The road, usually a conduit to progress, felt like an insurmountable barrier. But, beneath the surface, a seed of resilience began to germinate. Olivette squared her shoulders, wiped away a bead of sweat, and continued her journey on foot, determined to face the challenges head-on, even if the road proved a reluctant companion.

As Olivette traversed the winding roads, the sun dipped below the horizon, casting long shadows that stretched across her path. The second challenge presented itself as an elusive search for shelter. The quaint lights of a distant town twinkled like stars, promising a respite from the weariness of the road.

Finding safe and affordable shelter along the way emerged as a genuine concern. If she could not find transportation, she should at least be able to find a place to lay her head, or so she thought. It was a long road, and Olivette grappled with the need for accommodation. Securing a place to rest became a hurdle.

Olivette approached the outskirts of an inviting town. Fatigue clung to her like a heavy cloak, urging her to find a place to rest. The welcoming glow of streetlights and the distant murmur of life in the town held the promise of sanctuary. Olivette navigated the quiet streets using the flickering lights to find a hotel or sympathetic person willing to offer a spare room. Yet, as she inquired, the doors seemed to shut in her face, and the warm glow of hospitality turned cold.

Frustration mounted with each rejection, and Olivette's heart sank when she realized that finding shelter would be more challenging than expected. The distant echoes of laughter and music from a lively tavern were a haunting reminder of her outsider status.

Determined to find a place to rest her head, Olivette pressed on. The town square offered a semblance of serenity, and she noticed a humble inn nestled in a quiet corner. The flickering lights of a restaurant just close to the inn beckoned Olivette, offering a temporary refuge from the relentless downpour outside. The cozy interior was warm, a sharp contrast to the chilling whispers in her mind. She settled at a corner table, seeking solace in a warm bowl of soup.

As she spooned the soup, fragments of conversation drifted to her ears, hushed tones mingling with the clinking of cutlery. Suspicion settled upon Olivette as she caught snatches of the locals' discussions—whispers laden with an unsettling intent, a mysterious ritual that seemed to involve her presence. The hairs on her neck stood on end, and a shiver traversed her spine.

Trying to shake off the unease, Olivette called over to the waiter, hoping to glean some reassurance or clarity.

She leaned in slightly on the counter. "Excuse me, could you tell me anything about a ritual that happens here in this town? There seems to be some murmuring going on."

The waiter glanced around cautiously before responding, "Ah, you've noticed, haven't you? There are whispers about a sacred ritual carried out during these nights. But, Miss, it's best not to concern yourself with local gossip."

As she conversed with the waiter, a local approached her, wearing a friendly smile that seemed to contrast the ominous, hushed tones.

"Hello there! I haven't seen your face around these parts before. Need any help? We're a friendly bunch here, always ready to assist newcomers."

Despite his friendly demeanor, Olivette could tell there was something off about him. She could sense an underlying tension beneath the surface of cordiality.

She spoke politely, "Thank you. I'm just passing through, hoping for a night's rest. Is there any place nearby where I could find accommodation?"

The local hesitated for a moment, his gaze shifting, before he responded with a vague gesture toward the direction of the inn Olivette had noticed earlier. Smiling, he said, "The inn over there should be a suitable spot for travelers like yourself. They might have a room or two available."

Though the smiles were warm, Olivette couldn't shake the feeling that there was a hidden agenda beneath the facade of hospitality. The unsettling notion that the act was a part of something unknown gnawed at her, urging her to be cautious amidst the seemingly welcoming atmosphere of the town.

Fear ignited within Olivette as she realized the danger lurking in the shadows of the seemingly tranquil town. Without a second thought, she retreated into the anonymity of the night. The road now stretched out as a lifeline to escape the ominous town. As Olivette hurried into the night, the glow of the streetlights faded behind her, leaving the town's secrets concealed in the darkness. The second challenge had transformed a quest for shelter into a desperate flight from the unknown.

The unpredictability of the weather posed another challenge. From scorching heat to unexpected rainstorms, Olivette needed to adapt to the ever-changing climate. As she ventured further along the winding road, the third challenge unveiled itself in the weather's form. The skies, once serene, transformed into a tempestuous canvas, threatening to drench her in the unforgiving downpour.

The first droplets fell as gentle warnings, and then, like an orchestra building to a crescendo, the rain intensified. Now slick with precipitation, the road mirrored the challenges that seemed to intensify with each passing moment. Olivette pressed forward, her steps heavy with the weight of rain-soaked clothing and weary determination. The rhythmic pattering of raindrops played a dissonant melody on the road—slippery, and demanding unwavering resilience.

Desperation set in as Olivette sought refuge from the relentless onslaught. With no sign of shelter in sight, she cast a desperate glance around, searching for any respite. Then, like a beacon in the tempest, she spotted a dilapidated bus stop, its worn roof offering a modest shield from the storm.

Olivette huddled beneath the meager protection of the bus stop. The weathered structure creaked in protest against the wind, but it was a sanctuary against the elements. She peeled off her sodden jacket and put her head under it.

The rain, relentless in its pursuit, did not dampen Olivette's spirit. In the face of adversity, she drew strength from her faith, her hope, her desires, and her aspirations. The rain continued relentlessly. Olivette was cold, but she did not allow doubt to sink its ominous fingers into her mind. Her determination kept her warm, and the challenge served as a testament to her resilience.

"I'll weather this storm, Camile," she whispered, her voice a quiet vow against the sound of raindrops. The road ahead may have been sodden and uncertain, but each raindrop strengthened her resolve to continue on the journey. The third challenge became a chapter in Olivette's story, a tale of strength and fortitude against the tempest.

The journey brought Olivette into contact with a diverse array of people. While some of these interactions offered opportunities for connection, they also carried the challenge of discerning genuine intentions, navigating cultural differences, and safeguarding herself in unfamiliar environments. Her interactions were characterized by self-centeredness and a refusal to offer assistance.

With their faces hidden behind the shield of indifference, many drivers passed her by without giving her a second glance. The road seemed to stretch endlessly, and each ignored plea for help chipped away at Olivette's faith in the goodness of human beings. A few individuals stopped, attaching a price tag to offer their assistance. Their willingness to help was contingent on Olivette's financial capability, a stark reminder that altruism was a rare commodity on the road she traveled. Some offered their sympathy, fleetingly acknowledging Olivette's struggle with no genuine intention to help her out of her hardships. While seemingly supportive, their words held no substance, leaving her with an emptiness that mirrored the desolate stretches of the road.

As the journey continued, the weight of these encounters pressed heavily on Olivette's shoulders. The road, once a symbol of possibility, seemed to narrow into a tunnel of despair. Doubt crept in, and the allure of surrender became a seductive whisper in her ear.

In a moment of exhaustion and frustration, Olivette contemplated turning back. The relentless challenges, coupled with the indifference of those she encountered, fueled the temptation to retreat to the familiarity of Aunt May's farm. Memories of Camile's soft coos reminded her of the comforts of home. Yet faced with despair, a quiet resolve flickered within Olivette. She conjured an image of Camile, her innocent eyes reflecting trust in her strength. The road behind may have been littered with disappointing encounters, but the road ahead held the promise of the garden she sought—the garden that whispered promises of transformation and love.

With a deep breath, Olivette straightened her posture and adjusted the bag slung over her shoulder. The decision to press on became a declaration—an affirmation that the journey, despite its challenges and self-centered encounters, was a testament to her resilience and the untapped well of strength within. The road stretched before her, and each step became a defiance against the almost overwhelming allure of surrender.

"Transformation begins in the heart—where love's tender whispers encourage us to shed our past and step into the light of our true selves."

# 7

# *Transformation*

"Oh, finally," Olivette gasped. "I'm here."

She turned around, looking up into the sky. After hours of walking the lone road, she felt the vibrations of the leaf in her arms.

"Well done, dear child." She heard a voice whispering to her. Smiling with tears in her eyes, she jumped with jubilation. She bent low to catch her breath, exhausted from days without rest or food. When she raised her head, she came upon a bend and as she trudged on, she discovered a town reverberating with life.

"Food!" she cried as she raced towards the town.

As Olivette entered the town, she admired the hustle and bustle of life. "Finally," she said, "normal people." There was a sharp contrast between the lively town and the desolate paths she had traveled. The town was a refreshing departure from the eerie stillness of her recent encounters.

The air was filled with the savory aroma of street food and the harmonious cacophony of laughter and chatter. Stalls lined the streets, adorned with colorful fabrics and vibrant displays of produce, evidence of the locals' craftsmanship and livelihood.

People bustled about, their faces animated with joy, contemplation, a frown there, laughter, children running about, a mother calling her young children, a little banter here, a chatter there. It was the image of an imagined utopia. Children darted between market stalls, their laughter echoing through the lively streets. Olivette, overcome with relief, smiled at the beautiful sight.

Her fatigue melted away in the vibrant atmosphere, but hunger clawed at her stomach, and she followed the tantalizing scent of freshly cooked chicken. She walked to the aroma, which led her to a bustling eatery where the aroma emanated. Locals and travelers gathered, exchanging stories, and sharing the simple pleasures of a warm meal.

Seizing the opportunity, Olivette hurriedly approached the food stall, her stomach rumbling with hunger. The welcoming aroma wrapped around her, and she couldn't contain her excitement. Unsure that this wasn't another test, she listened for affirmation.

"Eat," the voice offered quietly.

"Phew!" she exclaimed with a mix of relief and elation, catching the attention of the stall's attendants. She ordered a hearty meal with a grateful heart, savoring the promise of nourishment and the welcoming warmth of the steam—a stark contrast to the challenges and uncertainties she had encountered on her journey thus far.

Amidst the vibrant bustle of the town, Olivette savored the flavors of the warm meal, finding solace in the hearty dish before her. As she ate, she struck up conversations with the townspeople, sharing snippets of her journey and listening intently to their tales.

"A young traveler, I see." A bald man walked up to her table.

"Yes, it's been a long journey."

Others heard and joined in.

"I bet you've seen many things," a woman offered.

"Phew. It's been a long, hard one!" she exclaimed, shaking her head animatedly. The locals burst into laughter, and she joined them.

The bald man was nodding now with a contemplative grin, spotting his face. "Ah, travelers often find respite here, but what brings you our way?"

"I am searching for something greater than me—answers, perhaps, or maybe a new beginning. But for tonight, I want shelter and a place to rest."

"You know what?" A young woman beckoned, "Your dinner is on me. You don't have to pay. I have an inn just across from this place. You bet you'll be getting a warm bed to lay your weary head on."

Olivette feared she was too trusting and waited for reassurance.

"You're safe," came the reassuring voice.

With gratitude, Olivette finished her meal and followed the local to her inn. True to her word, she took her to her inn. Its quaint exterior exuded a comforting charm, and as she entered, the cozy ambiance enveloped her with a welcoming embrace.

The innkeeper was cheerful and eager. "Watch your step," she said, guiding Olivette up the stairs of the inn.

Olivette, expressing gratitude, began, "I've been on the road for days without food or shelter. I almost lost any hope of finding good people to take me in."

"Oh yes, I have heard of many who thread this part. The other towns are way too hostile for a traveler like you. Lucky you didn't get lynched." She stopped when they got to the third floor. "Here is a room for you., it is cozy and welcoming."

The snug room had simple furnishings, a quilt, and a woolen blanket. Grateful for a safe place to spend the night, she settled in, reveling in the luxury of a soft bed and the promise of a restful sleep after days of exhaustion. Her heart felt lighter as she fell asleep peacefully as a result of the welcoming town's warmth and hospitality.

The next morning, she expressed her gratitude to the innkeeper, who was all too happy to feed her breakfast. The kindness of the locals overwhelmed Olivette. After breakfast, Olivette followed the leaf to the edge of town.

A connection was established when she placed the leaf between the Holy Book; it was like she could see things. She felt she could see her destination, and every step was confident. The journey led her to a place she had never been before—a realm of unfamiliarity and mystery. On the outskirts of the town, she could hear the hefty breath of the wind as she passed along a ridge. The lights from the town cast a curtain of ambiance in contrast with the silence of her current location.

She was wearing a brown turtle-neck top, matching it with brown cargo pants. *'It's going to be a long journey, and pockets were essential,'* she thought humorously. She wound a scarf tightly around her neck, balancing her backpack on her back. As she got to more sparse lands and the atmosphere became calmer, like the earth breathing freshness into her, she knew she was getting close.

In the wilderness, there were no inns where she could stop to spend the night, but surprisingly, she felt safe. Sometimes, she only had to lie down on a carpet of grass to pass the night under the evening stars. She felt an envelope of warmth every time she lay down to sleep, so the cold did not bother her. She was hardly hungry, too. Sometimes, she walked for days before stopping to rest or eat, yet she did not feel discouraged or too tired to move on. She only had a few cookies and bars of chocolate with her.

The leaf was leading her to a forest. She caught glimpses of it in her dreams—the garden was within the forest. When she slept, she could feel the luscious, tall grasses with her fingers, as if she were walking amidst them.

As she got closer to the forest, where the secrets of the garden awaited her, the dreams took a turn. Glimpses of a stranger emerged—a figure whose presence was intertwined with the path before her—a kaftan, dark wavy hair, and brown eyes. She felt the sparks of their connection. Each time she tried to reach this stranger; she was woken from her reverie. She felt the stranger beckon on her, too, but it seemed the threads of fate were not ready to bring them together.

Seeing her fellow dreamer reignited a fire within her. She was not alone. The divine had sent her a partner—a fellow traveler with whom she could share her desires and this journey toward self-discovery. She knew they could not meet yet, but she was in no hurry to do so. Like it or not, they would, so there was no rush.

As she got closer to the edge of the forest, she saw a heavy gate of twigs and trees. The closer she got, the tighter the air got. A menacing curtain of wind masked the entrance of the forest and almost sent her running back, but she knew she was supposed to be there. She wound her scarf tightly around her neck and pushed against the wind with her hands crossed in front of her. An inch away from the gate of twigs, she felt gigantic hands lift her and push her forward. She was now standing between the wind and the forest.

She was in a different realm.

As she settled and caught her breath, an opening appeared. A gust of wind raced past her and shot right through the opening, creating a path for her.

It was magic.

Through the gaping hole, the heavy sound of waterfalls and the twitters of birds flooded the air. Her face lit up with the eagerness of a toddler. She walked in, taking in the buzz of energy around her. Streaks of light dotted her path and formed ethereal patterns in the line-up of tall trees. Her steps were careful as if she did not want to disturb the fresh green grass or the sleeping birds in their nests. She did not know she was not alone until she heard a twig snap because she was so enamored with the beauty of the forest.

Startled, she turned sharply. A man whose eyes held a hint of wisdom and a smile that exuded warmth stood before her. He, too, seemed taken by the beauty of the forest but stopped when he saw her.

Like her, the voice and the leaf had drawn him on this enchanting journey. There was an instant connection between them as if their souls recognized each other from a distant past and an unlived future. They exchanged glances, their eyes searching for answers, both aware of the significance of their meeting. The leaf's energy seemed to pulse through Olivette, igniting a fire that resonated with their shared purpose. It was as if he felt it, too, because, at the exact moment, he stared down at his hands. They extended their fingertips in each other's direction as if on instinct. The closer they got, the stronger the energy pulsed in their veins, so they stepped a safe distance away, unsure what would happen if they allowed their hands to touch.

"You heard the voice too, didn't you?" Olivette asked, her voice filled with wonder.

The man nodded, a smile playing on his lips. "Yes, I did. It called for me to follow the leaf. I'm guessing the same as you."

Silence.

"I'm Nazam."

*'Nazam.'* The name sounded so familiar as if she knew whom it belonged to, yet she was sure she did not know anyone who went by the name.

"Olivette," she said, seeing the flicker of recognition in his eyes.

"I think we've met without knowing it."

"Maybe." Olivette tried to shrug off the feeling of familiarity. "I only remember glimpses of a man that looked like you."

"I admit to seeing the resemblance of a lady like you."

Olivette took in his appearance. He was an Indian with a slender figure, wearing a dark blue sweatshirt with cargo pants similar to hers. His long hair was midnight black, falling on both sides of his face. His nonchalant appearance spoke of the length and trouble of his journey. "What can you remember? What did she have on?"

"A blue sequin dress- like a Cinderella dress."

"Hmmm." Olivette had only ever worn anything like that in her dreams. She never went to prom, so there was no reason for her to have worn such a dress, but she could imagine it. She had seen that dress many times—a light blue ball gown with sequin details and feather fittings at the hems.

"Well, I saw a man in a brown kaftan. Brown eyes—just the eyes."

Nazam chuckled. "I have brown eyes, but a kaftan? I haven't worn that in years."

They both laughed at the absurdity of their visions. Their hearts beat in unison, and their souls intertwined in a dance of a newfound connection. They stood there, united by a common purpose and bound by the invisible thread of destiny. Together, they resolved to continue their journey, to follow the scent of love to the location that had been revealed to them. They had been destined to find each other and embark on this journey of love together.

"What now?" Olivette inquired.

Like an answer to her question, the leaf's energy pulsed within her and she could see Nazam felt it too. As if on cue, they reached out their fingertips. Just a touch. They heard the faint buzz of current pass through their veins.

The pulse became stronger and stronger until the fingers touched each other's fingers.

Suddenly, sparks of light traveled through their veins, stunning them, and putting them in a one-second trance. In front of them, a fresh path opened up to reveal paved ground.

"I think we're supposed to follow the path."

"No kidding," Nazam answered with a hint of sarcasm.

Hand in hand, Olivette and Nazam ventured deeper into the forest. The leaf led them through the lush forests and babbling brooks, each step bringing them closer to the place where they would be healed. They shared stories, dreams, and aspirations, finding solace in each other's presence.

"This is the strangest thing I've ever experienced," Nazam said as they crossed a river. "I was at work when I saw my first vision. When I came, I was sitting in a dumpster."

Olivette burst into laughter. "What? That's more interesting than when I found myself in the middle of my street."

As the days turned into weeks, they grew closer. They reveled in the beauty of nature and in the serenity of their shared experiences. Love blossomed between them, a love that was both familiar and new. It was a love that transcended boundaries and cultures, nurtured by the magic of their journey.

Finally, after a treacherous climb up a towering mountain, they reached a massive gate guarded by guards dressed in regal attire. The guards watched as Olivette and Nazam approached, their eyes sharp and vigilant. Olivette and Nazam exchanged a knowing look, their hearts filled with excitement and trepidation.

"I think this is it," Olivette said, her voice filled with determination. Unlike her, Nazam didn't seem so excited. He was cautious.

"These guards look fierce."

"Oh, don't worry, Nazam. We've been expecting you." One of the guards said, His kind smile held the wisdom of years and many lives. He seemed like a man who had traversed time and space. The guard had white hair pouring like reeds from the headgear on his head—a gold headband with strange inscriptions.

The second guard looked on, observing the conversation with an air of awareness. His hair was white, too, but with streaks of gray here and there. He seemed younger than the one who spoke to them. Looking between the two new visitors, he admitted they were special. No one of their age had ever answered the call, and he was surprised they had made it so far.

Taken aback by the mention of his name, Nazam gulped, his eyes gleaming with the reflection of the guards' plates. Olivette did not share Nazam's fear, so she stepped forward and bowed, as she had seen in those Gladiator films at home.

The white-haired guard burst into laughter while the other stepped back, surprised by Olivette's gesture.

"You don't have to do that," they said in unison.

"Oh," Olivette said, her cheeks were hot with embarrassment. "It seemed like the right thing to do."

"No."

After a brief pause, the younger guard took a few steps back. "Nazam, Olivette. Welcome." He stretched his hands toward the gates.

The colossal gates stood before them, bearing marks of the passage of time, a shield for the mysteries that lay in the sacred space beyond. They loomed tall, their once gleaming surface now weathered with age, etched with ancient symbols that seemed to pulsate faintly in the light.

With a resounding creak that echoed through the air, the gates stirred, a slow and deliberate movement like the awakening of a long-dormant titan. Each hinge groaned in protest against the weight they bore, sending vibrations through the ground beneath their feet.

Nazam's breath hitched in anticipation, his gaze fixed on the gates as they slowly parted, revealing what lay beyond. A palpable tension hung in the air, intertwining with a sense of reverence and awe. Olivette gasped with the movement, mouth agape, as she anticipated what was behind the gate. As the gates' movement slowed against the loud protest of their hinges, it amplified the anticipation that swirled within Nazam and Olivette.

For both Nazam and Olivette, the gates' slow motion ignited a mixture of curiosity and trepidation. The anticipation built with each fraction of an inch the gates yielded, hinting at an enigmatic realm that lay beyond—a place promising answers, enlightenment, and a transformative journey.

The gates creaked and vibrated.

Olivette and Nazam held their breaths, unsure of what awaited them on the other side. But they were prepared to face any challenge and embrace the unknown, fueled by the connection they now shared.

And so Olivette and Nazam continued their journey, their hearts filled with hope and anticipation. They knew that beyond the gates lay a world where their love would be celebrated, where dreams would come true, and where their destinies would be forever entwined.

With a deep exhale, Olivette and Nazam stepped forward, ready to cross the threshold into a world with the promise of love, enchantment, and unimaginable beauty. Their journey had only begun, but they knew they were destined to uncover the secrets beyond the gates and find the garden that awaited them.

"Beyond the gate lies a world where dreams are nurtured, and love's magic touches every corner of our being."

# 8

# The Enchanted Gate

"Look," she exclaimed to her companion, "behold the truly awe-inspiring city before us!"

The city stretched like a vast drapery of dreams, saturated in shades that exceeded earthly comparisons. Pale blues and soft lavenders of twilight blended seamlessly in the city, giving the impression that it was dancing to the tones of celestial dawn. Towering crystalline structures, kissed by the glow of distant stars, reached toward an endless sky.

Radiant, luminous bridges, suspended in mid-air, connected ethereal spires adorned with sparkling symbols. Though intricate and grand, the cityscape had an air of weightless grace, like the cosmic artistry of an unseen architect. Gardens of blooms adorned floating platforms, their petals reflecting the soft glow of the lights that bathed the city. Cascading waterfalls, seemingly defying gravity, flowed from crystalline cliffs, their waters imbued with liquid luminescence.

The city carried the harmony of otherworldly forces, a masterpiece that unfolded before Olivette and Nazam like a dream untethered from the constraints of reality. The air carried a faint melody—a hum that resonated with the energy of the city itself.

Olivette and Nazam, their eyes wide with awe, felt as if they had stepped into a realm where the boundaries of the mundane dissolved and the wonders of the world unveiled themselves in a symphony of colors and lights. They were drawn to the celestial city, unblemished by the passage of time, enticed by the mysteries it held and eager to uncover the cosmic truths that lay within its gleaming embrace.

"Greetings," a voice boomed, "seekers of the celestial realm," his voice resonating with a deep, melodic cadence. "I am Amazel, your guide within these sacred walls."

The resonance of his voice seemed to ripple through the air, a harmonious vibration that stirred the celestial city around them. Olivette and Nazam swiveled from their enraptured gaze, turning their attention toward the source of the voice.

Amazel stepped into view as his words echoed, his presence an ethereal celestial radiance. His attire, a cascade of flowing robes, mirrored the colors of a cosmic sunrise—soft pastels blending seamlessly with luminescent whites, creating an ever-shifting spectrum that defied earthly comparisons. His apparel shimmered with cosmic colors that outdid earthly comparisons. The fabric was a luminescent silver, like moonlight dancing on water, interwoven with tinges of twilight blues and velvety purples.

Olivette and Nazam, entranced by the sight before them, realized that the colors of Amazel's clothing weren't like anything Olivette and Nazam had seen before. They were shades and tones from a supernatural palette that cast an otherworldly glow on Amazel's face. There were few words to accurately describe his face.

Amazel's face was a tarp of eccentric proportions and seemed to carry secrets of ages and the benevolence of a god. His deep eyes held understanding—a gaze that seemed to reach into Olivette and Nazam's souls. His features were chiseled with timeless wisdom, radiating a glow that matched the light surrounding them. They bore a kindness that softened the enormity of his presence.

Amazel stood tall and regal, with earthly strength and celestial grace. The lights played in his hair, pouring down like liquid stardust strands, giving him an otherworldly aura. His hands moved with elegance as he spoke. Every movement, deliberate and fluid, left trails of shimmering stardust in the air—a celestial choreography that accompanied his words.

The celestial guide's stature, neither imposing nor aloof, almost made him approachable, and his energy, like a celestial breeze, embraced Olivette and Nazam. His presence invited them to explore the absurdities of a celestial existence.

Amazel moved even closer to them now.

"I am Amazel," he repeated, his voice a celestial melody that hung in the air, "and I shall be your guide."

He spread his hands towards the city and smiled at them. "What is it that you seek?"

Olivette, her eyes filled with wonder and determination, replied, "We were sent here, called in our dreams and visions."

Nazam continued, "We seek enlightenment, a deeper understanding of the mysteries that intertwine the celestial and the human."

Amazel nodded knowingly. "If I could count the number of times a human has said that, we'd be here for ages." His eyes danced between Olivette and Nazam. "So, what does enlightenment mean to you?" he asked with a graceful smile, his eyes twinkling with age and wisdom.

With Amazel's gaze piercing yet compassionate, Nazam spoke, picking up his words carefully. "It is the illumination of the soul, a communion with the divine, and the realization of our interconnectedness with all creation."

Amazel nodded. "Enlightenment is a path of unveiling a journey that transcends the boundaries of the known." His eyes sparked with the intensity of his words. "Enlightenment is not a destination; it is an ongoing revelation. Follow me, and I will lead you through, where the threads of your destinies are woven."

As they walked through corridors with celestial symbols inscribed into pillars, Amazel continued, "Enlightenment is not the acquisition of knowledge alone. It is the fusion of wisdom and love, the harmonious resonance of one's soul with another; a cosmic symphony."

The celestial palace, with its intricate passages and profound teachings, unfolded before Olivette and Nazam.

Olivette, remembering her encounters, stated, "You know how we got here. You know our story." She looked toward Nazam, acknowledging that he had a story to tell. "I left my family to be here because I wish to understand the essence of life. Without question and with an open heart, Amazel, I want to be transformed." She let her words settle into meaning. "I hope to find not just answers but also to restore the love within my soul."

Amazel smiled at Olivette's words, admiring her resilience. He had indeed witnessed her journey to this point. The answers they sought would come to them in time, but it was not his pace to show them how. He was a mere guide, more like a tour guide. He commended her for her intuition. "Yes, Olivette, and that is what you will find—answers."

He gestured toward the city below. "The celestial city. Like the city itself, the threads of your journey are woven into the cosmic tapestry."

Olivette felt a profound sense of belonging. "It's breathtaking, Amazel."

"Love is the mender of all wounds. In the celestial city, where every light is a soul finding its way, redemption is possible and inherent in the very fabric of existence."

Nazam, a silent observer, nodded in agreement. The celestial city offered a backdrop to their conversation—a witness to the mysteries of their journey with the celestial realm.

"Love, in its purest form, transcends time and forgives all transgressions," Amazel continued.

"As you seek enlightenment, you will find the keys to unlock the chambers of your heart and release the healing energies within. But you must be ready to pull your weight and do the grunt of the work."

Olivette lingered on the last words. Of course, she knew they would have to work, but she wondered if it was anything like the challenges she faced on her way. She looked at Nazam, wondering whether he had the same thoughts as her.

As Olivette, Nazam, and Amazel delved deeper, the city began to morph. The towering crystal structures gave way to a familiar sight—the enchanting garden Olivette had encountered in her dreams and Nazam in his visions.

"What is going on?" Olivette asked.

Amazel spoke, his voice carrying the weight of what he was about to say, gently urging them to listen. "The celestial city is only an apparition, a reflection of what lies deep within you. The true essence of your journey begins here."

Before them, the celestial city was melting, revealing more and more of the garden. It parted like a curtain, revealing a garden that seemed to echo with the whispers of unseen wonders. Olivette and Nazam, though familiar with the concept of the garden, found themselves standing on the threshold of an experience that exceeded the boundaries of their understanding.

Amazel, with a knowing smile, gestured toward the garden.

"This," he began, "is where the celestial truths intertwine with the roots of your being. Let the garden unfold its secrets and seekers embrace the journey of transformation."

He explained the reason behind the celestial city's apparition. "The city, a shimmering tangle of dreams, was a manifestation of your collective visions—a bridge between the known and the unknown. It served as a celestial guidepost, a beacon that drew you closer to the garden, where the roots of your journey await."

Amazel's words carried a wisdom that resonated with the cosmic forces at play. His voice started to tremble as he spoke, just like a far-away echo that the celestial breeze had carried away. "You have reached the peak of your journey."

The vibrant colors of his robes started to lose their luster, blending with the surroundings. The celestial city, once a beacon of dreams, waned, and with it, Amazel and the celestial guards dissolved into the fabric of the fading illusion.

Olivette and Nazam watched in quiet awe as the figures before them became mere echoes. Amazel's parting words lingered in the air as the celestial guards, nodding their acknowledgment, joined the dissolution.

The once-vibrant garden, now the sole reality, embraced the fading remnants of the celestial city, reclaiming its place as the focal point of their journey. The shock of witnessing the disappearance of Amazel and the celestial guards settled on them with an understanding—the celestial city, the celestial guide, and the guards were transient guides on a journey that transcended the boundaries of the ethereal realm. The garden beckoned them to unravel its mysteries and continue the transformative journey that awaited within its embrace.

The disappearing apparitions prompted them to reflect. Olivette and Nazam questioned the nature of their journey, wondering what symbolism they were to gather. The city was guiding them to this pivotal moment.

As the city dissolved along with Amazel and the guards, a thick fog took its place, blinding the two travelers from seeing the garden. When the mist cleared, Olivette and Nazam felt a quiet fall on them. Blinking the fog away, they squinted to see what was before them.

"Oh! No!" Nazam reacted.

"It's gone!" Olivette exclaimed.

As the mist dissipated, the garden materialized before Olivette and Nazam. However, it was not the vibrant haven they had seen in their dreams. Instead, it was a dark and dreary landscape, a stark contrast from the lush and luminous scenes etched in their minds. It was merely the skeleton of their luscious dreamscape.

The garden stood before them like a mere echo—a skeleton of the garden in the dreams they had carried. The glow that once emanated from the blooms had given way to shadows that clung to the twisted branches of skeletal trees. The flowers, once radiant with iridescent colors, now hung their heads, their petals casting a somber shadow on the dimly lit ground.

Olivette's eyes widened with disbelief, her expression a canvas of astonishment painted with strokes of disappointment. She exchanged a glance with Nazam, whose features mirrored her disbelief. The garden, once a symbol of hope and transformation, had transformed into a melancholic realm that seemed to mirror the shadows within Olivette and Nazam's regrets.

"No, it's the same one," Olivette said, her voice a whisper that hung in the air. She had a resigned look that reflected the disappointment she felt. Nazam, grappling with an equal sense of disbelief, nodded in silent acknowledgment.

"It looks like the skeleton of the one we saw in our dreams."

The atmosphere shifted. The air in the darkened garden carried a heavy stillness, interrupted only by the faint rustle of leaves. The celestial lights that had once illuminated their dreams now flickered, casting an eerie presence over the scene. The contrast between their expectations and the grim state of the garden weighed on Olivette and Nazam.

"If this is what we were meant to find, then what is our purpose? What is the point of the journey? What are we to do with this?" Nazam voiced the question that lingered unspoken between them.

Olivette could only offer a shrug; her brow furrowed, deepening the lines etched on her forehead. Their journey had taken an unexpected turn, plunging them into the depths of a garden that mirrored the shadows within their souls.

Uncertainty clung to the air as they stood amidst the darkened garden, seeping into the uncharted territories of their fears and doubts. The path ahead, once clear in their dreams, now unfolded as a twisted and winding trail, beckoning them to explore the mysteries that awaited in the heart of the unexpected celestial realm.

"This is the current state of your hearts." A faint whisper came to them, echoing through the desolate expanse of the darkened garden.

As fear seized their hearts, they turned around, searching for the voice now speaking to them. The ethereal voice, like the one that had guided them in their dreams, carried wisdom that transcended the shadows. The voice seemed to emanate from every part of the garden, bearing the resemblance of the broken state of the landscape. It was like a revelation unfolding amidst the somber scene.

"The garden mirrors the state of your souls," the voice continued, weaving through the skeletal branches and lingering in the air like a celestial melody. "Just as it stands in the shadows, so do your hearts. The journey you seek is not only through celestial blooms but also through the shadows within your souls."

Realization dawned on Olivette and Nazam. The unexpected transformation of the garden, from a realm of vibrant dreams to a realm of shadows, echoed the complexities of their inner turmoil. The celestial journey, it seemed, was not just about basking in the radiance of ethereal beauty but also about navigating the shadows that resided within their hearts.

Nazam absorbed the wisdom of the celestial voice and nodded in silent acknowledgment. The garden, cloaked in shadows, projected significance—a reflection of their inner landscapes, with light and darkness interwoven.

As the celestial voice faded, leaving behind a hushed stillness, Olivette and Nazam found themselves pondering their next steps.

# 9

## The Hidden Treasure

Their journey had taken a different turn. It wasn't at all what they envisioned, but they were willing to explore their possibilities. They had reached their destination, yet they were told they had only just gotten to the task required of them.

Olivette whispered, her voice heavy with disappointment, "This... this is not what we anticipated."

Among the desolate gardens, Olivette and Nazam stood, their expectations shattered by the grim reality that lay before their eyes. The once vibrant and lush dreamscape they had envisioned was now a haunting echo of its former self, made even more apparent by the memory of the city that had just dissolved. Desolation—withering vegetation, bare pathways, and an eerie silence hanging in the air—had marred the formerly lush landscape. The very essence of the garden seemed tainted by lingering despair, a stark contrast to the vibrant haven they had dreamed of.

Their hearts sank in unison, grappling with the disillusionment that confronted them. The reality starkly contrasted with the visions that had guided their journey, leaving them bewildered and at a loss for explanation. Yet, amidst the desolation, a faint glimmer of hope persisted. Determination flickered in their eyes as they vowed to uncover the truth behind the garden's current state while seeking enlightenment.

Nazam looked around, sullen and still in shock. "It's as if life had been drained from this place," he continued pensively, "but it is as the voice said. This is a mirror of our souls. It reflects just how we feel. We need to focus on restoring it—restoring our souls, the state of our minds."

Olivette sighed heavily. "Yes," she agreed.

An ancient tree stood alone at the center of the desolate landscape, its towering form a mirror of the passage of time and its resilience. An unexplainable pull—a magnetic force beckoning them closer—drew Olivette and Nazam cautiously toward it.

"It's magnificent. There's something here, something big." Olivette observed.

Nazam's eyes widened with wonder. "I can feel it too."

The tree's gnarled trunk bore scars etched with intricate patterns like runes, telling stories of others who had been here before them. Its weathered branches, bearing rough patches from exposure to the elements, swayed gently and cast shimmering rays of light on the ground.

As they approached, the air seemed to crackle with a strange force, an unseen current that filled them with anticipation and reverence. The soft glow surrounding the tree pulsed rhythmically, like a heartbeat through the garden.

"There's something hidden within this tree. Love led us here for a reason, Nazam," Olivette said, hoping to paint the cadence of her voice.

Nazam nodded in agreement. "We need to uncover the truth and the wisdom this tree holds. It feels like a beacon in this desolation."

With hands interlaced and hearts filled with determination, Olivette and Nazam stood before the ancient tree, ready to unlock the mysteries and treasures hidden within its enigmatic embrace. They braced themselves, ready to delve deeper into the secrets that awaited them, hoping to unearth the wisdom to illuminate their path.

The faint sound of movement caught Olivette and Nazam's attention as they exchanged troubled glances. Their eyes widened in alarm when they spotted two figures lying on the ground, barely conscious and struggling to regain their bearings.

Olivette rushed forward, "Are you okay? What happened?"

The pair appeared fatigued, their faces etched with exhaustion and distress. They seemed disoriented with labored breaths, like people who had run a marathon. Olivette and Nazam hurried to their side.

"Can you hear us? What happened here?"

The pair groaned softly, trying to gather their strengths and make sense of their surroundings. When they spoke, their voices trembled.

"Beware. This place is not as it seems. Illusions and despair lurk in the garden as much as the hope and beauty that it contains."

Olivette and Nazam exchanged worried glances. The cryptic warnings of the travelers hinted at hidden dangers within the garden, prompting a sense of caution and apprehension. But it also meant that there were hidden treasures. Nazam and Olivette vowed within themselves to focus on the treasures rather than fear the dangers.

Olivette replied softly, "Rest now. We'll do what we can to help."

The two figures stirred, their strength slowly returning to them.

"I am Adam, the first man," the man spoke, his voice taking on a different tone as if he had not just relayed an ominous message.

"And I am Eve."

Nazam's eyes widened. "Adam... Eve?"

Olivette was astonished. "How... how can this be?"

"So, what is going on here?" Adam struggled to sit up.

"It's... it's like a dream." Eve gazed around in awe. "Adam, do you remember the last time we were here?"

"Such a long time."

They were taking in the scenery before them.

Olivette and Nazam exchanged incredulous glances as the strangers regained their bearings, their eyes holding a sense of recognition. The strangers nodded, their expressions a mix of disbelief and wonder at the unforeseen reunion.

Nazam was the first to chip in, "We've been searching... seeking answers for so long."

"Do you, maybe, know us? The leaf? This garden." Olivette said, waving at the garden.

Adam and Eve smiled knowingly. "We understand how you must feel. It is the same as the others before you."

The leaf Olivette carried began radiating a gentle glow, casting a soothing aura around them. It seemed to pulse with newfound energy as if responding to the presence of Adam and Eve.

"The leaf." They both chorused.

Nazam and Olivette gasped in unison.

"It's responding to them," Adam said. "We will be your guides in this garden." He assured them.

"But it is barely a garden," Nazam objected. "Our dreams were so much different from what we see now. How can you still smile like that? This is Eden, isn't it?"

"Indeed, it is," Eve replied, "or at least, it was until we were cast out."

"We only returned to serve as guides to new travelers," Adam added.

"So, you didn't die." I thought sin summoned death the minute you were out of here."

"Yes." Adam's eyes crinkled with wisdom. "But you know, no man truly dies. Our bodies died, yes, but being the first people, our souls transcend generations, guiding our children in their dreams through visions, hoping that they do not make the mistake that we did."

"But" Olivette protested.

"But humans will be humans, yes." Eve completed her sentence for her: "And there's only so much we can do."

"Come, give us your leaves." Adam and Eve stretched out their arms towards Nazam and Olivette.

For the first time since entering the garden, Olivette put her backpack down as she took out her Bible. She gently extended the leaf toward Adam and Eve. The faint glow intensified, enveloping the strangers in a luminous embrace. Nazam had his in a little vial wrapped in brown clothing. Adam and Eve took the leaves and threw them into their mouths. Slowly, the vitality returned to Adam and Eve as they chewed, their features becoming more defined as if awakening from a long slumber.

Adam's muscles reverberated with an extra glow, and Eve's skin seemed to glow like the sun. The electric current that flows between Nazam and Olivette now swirled in circular motions around Adam and Eve.

The force pulled Nazam and Olivette together, they saw the passing of time—from the fall of man in the Garden of Eden to the birth of Joseph and the fall of Jericho. They saw the birth and death of Jesus, and their eyes filled with tears. At that point, the swirl became stronger, Jesus' pain making it a more potent force. They felt so lucky to be recipients of such vivid apparitions. They saw war unfold and the debris of starvation and disease as they wrecked the world.

Olivette saw her mother and her daughter in Louisville. She saw the people of Louisville, oblivious to the turmoil that had eaten into the depths of the world. As the vibrant colors continued to dance around them, Nazam felt a wave of memories rush over him—memories that had lingered in the corners of his mind for years. Nazam saw his father at his shop and his family holding meetings. His eyes filled with tears when he saw their faces. It had been gone too long.

Olivette cried out, "Our souls... I can see your memories," she beamed. "We are more powerful than we know."

Their love—separate entities within themselves—bloomed with a fiery force. It was a pure and enduring force that seemed to transform them. It was not merely a fleeting emotion but a profound energy capable of healing and restoration. They were bonded now, and they understood that their bond held the power to infuse beauty and vitality into the most barren of landscapes, much like the garden had bloomed in response to their presence.

As the twirl slowly waned, Olivette and Nazam vibrated softly with the leaf's energy. They trembled with a newfound fervor and sank into the sand, clutching at their chests and weeping uncontrollably.

Nazam gazed into the distance and said, "My father... he was a strict traditionalist. Our Indian heritage and customs meant everything to him."

Olivette was listening intently. "What happened to him?"

"I didn't fit into his mold," Nazam spoke with a hint of sorrow in his voice. "My dreams clashed with his expectations. He wanted me to follow the path he had carved out for me."

"But that's not what you wanted," Eve said.

"Exactly," Nazam replied. "I yearned for freedom, to pursue my ambitions, and to explore beyond the boundaries he'd set. It led to endless clashes." Nazam recounted his restless struggle and the strife between his aspirations and his father's traditional ideals. His longing for autonomy and his father's unyielding expectations had driven a rift that seemed insurmountable.

Nazam wanted to pursue an academic path with dedication and excellence—completing a higher education degree. He aspired to do something outside the traditional courses of study, such as arts, humanitarian, or non-conventional sciences, driven by his passion for different forms of expression and his curiosity about non-conventional disciplines. His father, however, wanted him to pursue something along the lines of medicine, engineering, law, or business—potentially pushing him into a highly regarded field in their community. These fields were commonly revered in society for the stability, prestige, and potential financial security they provided.

His father also wanted him to be more active in the community and show more face at cultural events, festivals, and religious ceremonies, honoring and preserving their traditions. This would have included contributions to community organizations or volunteering for cultural causes.

While appreciating his heritage, Nazam wanted to engage with his culture more personally. His father did not like his 'new' ideas. Nazam liked to explore other cultures, finding their similarities and connections. He was exploring new ways to serve his community and celebrate their traditions while embracing modern perspectives and personal growth.

"Why not the conventional way?" his father asked him once. He argued that what Nazam was doing would do nothing to preserve their heritage and traditions but potentially ruin their credibility. "Our family carries a legacy that spans generations. Our traditions, our values—we can't just throw them all away."

Nazam recalled this conversation as having been the trajectory that called him to reflect on what he wanted for himself. It was this conversation that drove him into isolation, a dark pit of unforgiveness, and ultimately led him to seek ways of transformation.

"But, Father, I have dreams that extend beyond our heritage. I want to explore and chart my course," he remembered, standing across from his father under a lamppost.

His father had given him a curt reply: "Your dreams should align with our culture, not stray from it. Education, a respectable profession—these are your responsibilities."

He, however, was just as stubborn as his father—unwavering. "But what if my aspirations lie elsewhere? What if my calling isn't within those confines?"

"Your calling is here to uphold our legacy. Your dreams can't supersede our family's honor."

Nazam's father's expectations carried the weight of their tradition and cultural heritage, bearing down on his son's shoulders. The clash of dreams versus duty, freedom versus familiarity obligations, had been a recurrent theme in their exchanges. It was an insurmountable clash, pushing Nazam to seek liberation beyond the confines of his home.

His father expected him to contribute to the family's welfare and respect hierarchical family structures, which he understood. However, the fervor with which he was expected to perform was ridiculously extravagant, which he could not afford.

"I tried my best. I did," Nazam said, exhaling. If he had stayed at home, his career choice would likely have been dictated. They would have compelled him to consider an esteemed profession within their culture or join the family business.

While these expectations were rooted in the preservation of tradition and family honor, Nizam's desire for personal freedom and a path of self-discovery led him to explore beyond his familiar boundaries, seeking his own identity and purpose, which differed from the predetermined path his father had set.

"It all became too suffocating. I had to break free. That's why I left home... to seek my path."

Olivette, placing a comforting hand on his shoulder, whispered, "Sometimes, our journeys take us far from where we began."

"Indeed. And in seeking that freedom, I've found myself here, with you, in this garden," he said with a smile.

As the memories of his past wove into the vibrant shades of the garden, Nazam realized that his quest for freedom and self-identity had led him to this transformative moment. It served as a testament to the resilient, yearning, and insatiable spirit that resided within him.

Eve looked at him with understanding and said, "Love has a remarkable ability to awaken life and restore hope. It's a force that transcends boundaries."

Adam bellowed his agreement: "Your love is a beacon, illuminating the path to hidden treasures within and around you."

Realization hit them. Olivette and Nazam would have to embrace the truth that their love would transform them. It was capable of turning barrenness into vibrant life and desolation into thriving beauty. It was a reminder that love, in its purest form, possessed an extraordinary power—an eternal source of healing, restoration, and endless possibilities.

"We are connected."

The garden echoed with a silent hum, a harmonious resonance that acknowledged the new union. A newfound vitality coursed through their veins, invigorating their limbs. Adam and Eve, revitalized by the leaf's mystical energy, gazed at Olivette and Nazam with concern. With a sense of purpose, they gestured towards Olivette and Nazam to start their journey through the labyrinth paths of the desolate garden.

Nazam gently squeezed Olivette's hand and nodded. Turning to Adam and Eve, he asked, "What do we do now?"

Adam beckoned, "Come, there's much to uncover."

Eve commented, "Now, we share desires, our pain, a gift granted us by the balm of life, the tree in the middle of the garden." She pointed towards the tall old tree at the center. "The garden holds many secrets hidden within its forgotten corners."

Olivette and Nazam followed closely, their senses heightened by the enigmatic aura that enveloped the garden. The ancient trees whispered ancient tales, and the faint echo of distant whispers seemed to guide their path as if the garden itself were steering them toward a revelation.

As they delved deeper, the garden transformed around them. The desolate wasteland began to shimmer with faint signs of life. Lush vegetation sprouted along the once-barren pathways, and vibrant blooms blossomed, adorning the landscape with shades unseen before.

Olivette cried in awe, "It's... it's changing."

Adam shook his head. "No. It is your souls that are changing. Because your souls are now blended, you see the same things."

Olivette cast a look towards Nazam, remembering the pictures of his family and feeling the pain he felt. She held out a hand to him, patting his shoulder gently.

"The garden is only awakening from a long slumber. Like your soul, it is beginning to feel the awesome power of God's grace."

The ethereal glow intensified, casting a radiant luminescence over the surroundings. The air seemed charged with an ineffable energy, guiding their steps toward a destination unknown yet undeniably significant.

"This way. The heart of the garden lies ahead." Eve continued, "There, the wisdom and truth you seek await."

With Adam and Eve leading the way, Olivette and Nazam pressed forward, their hearts brimming with anticipation and hope. They moved through the changing garden under the influence of an enigmatic force that was leading them in the direction of the mysterious realm's elusive heart, where they would find untold revelations and untapped wisdom.

Adam and Eve led Olivette and Nazam through the garden's evolving landscape, and the transformative power of the mystical realm unfolded before them. Lush greenery flourished where desolation had once reigned supreme, a testament to the garden's miraculous restorative ability.

Olivette could not mask her amusement. "It's unbelievable. The way the garden is rejuvenating itself... It's almost surreal."

Nazam nodded in amazement. "Indeed. Nature's resilience is awe-inspiring."

Adam and Eve stopped abruptly at the foot of a small tree. "This is where you must toil to restore the garden. What you see are only flashes of what you will achieve in the coming days."

Frowning, Olivette and Nazam stepped away from Adam and Eve, snapping around to see the garden fluctuate between its desolate state and the facade of its restoration.

Each step they took seemed to imbue the air with newfound vitality. The soft rustle of leaves carried the sweet scent of blossoms, filling them with renewed hope and purpose for what they would accomplish.

Eve said, "The garden does have a way of healing, restoring life to its very essence, but this journey will be nothing if you do nothing." Continuing, she said, "The garden represents your love and combined strength now, and you must both work to renew it."

The message resonated with Olivette and Nazam, making them optimistic amidst their challenging quest. The subtle glimmer of hope in their eyes mirrored the garden's resurgence, a symbolic reflection of their journey toward enlightenment.

As they ventured deeper into the heart of the garden, the four companions were enveloped in a serene ambiance, their hearts uplifted by the expectation of rejuvenation. The garden's transformative power would heal the land and rekindle a spark of optimism and determination within Olivette and Nazam, strengthening their resolve to uncover the mysteries that awaited them.

Eve touched Nazam's shoulder. "The garden responds to the hearts of those who seek its wisdom and love, and that little tree holds the essence of life and renewal."

The realization dawned on Olivette: "The leaves... they came from this tree."

"Yes. Not the old tree as we had thought." Nazam crouched and touched the bark of the tree, resulting in a green luminescent light sprouting from the roots and surrounding the tree. When he moved his hand away, the tree went back to normal.

"I told you we were connected; everyone and all the lives in this garden." Adam pointed at the small tree and said, "It's your soul tree."

In this breathtaking spectacle, Olivette and Nazam realized the profound connection they shared with the garden. The leaves were tokens of the tree's boundless vitality and the garden's innate ability to respond to the seekers' intentions and emotions.

Olivette and Nazam stood by the blossoming tree in awe of the stunning display of nature's magnificence. The garden unveiled its secrets before their very eyes, offering them a glimpse into the profound mysteries yet to be unveiled.

Olivette and Nazam realized that this journey was about discovering external treasures and unlocking their hearts' hidden depths. Love had brought them here, and their love breathed life back into the forgotten garden.

As they continued to explore, they stumbled on hidden paths leading to secret nooks and crannies filled with enchantment. They discovered sparkling waterfalls cascading into crystal-clear pools, where magical creatures frolicked joyfully. They found ancient manuscripts and paintings, capturing stories and wisdom from generations past. Each discovery filled their hearts with awe and gratitude for their journey.

But amid all the wonders, Olivette and Nazam realized the veritable treasure that lay in their connection. Their love could transform the most desolate places into havens of beauty and life. It was a reminder that love is not just a fleeting feeling but a force capable of healing and restoring.

As they hugged one another in the thriving garden they had revived, Olivette and Nazam realized that this journey was not just about the material treasures they had found but also about the eternal treasure they had discovered within themselves—a love that could dispel any gloom and bring light to Olivette in the most remote regions of the world.

With renewed determination, they vowed that they would put all their might into transforming the garden. The garden, once lost, had now become a testament to the power of love and the infinite possibilities that awaited those who dared to follow its path.

*"Restoration is the soul's return to wholeness—a journey back to love, where every wound is healed and every heartache fades."*

# 10

## The Restoration

"Oh, my God. Look at this!" Olivette called Nazam.

As the early hours of dawn set on them in the tranquility of the garden, Eve and Adam led Olivette and Nazam to consider their tasks in the garden.

Every part of the garden held meaning as if the garden itself were leading them to a new understanding of themselves. Now that they understood that the garden represented their interlaced souls, they understood the task that was ahead of them. They each imagined their souls being beautiful, clean, and free, anticipating the beginning of their restoration assignment.

They came across a small pond that was still and calm. Looking into its glassy surface, their eyes met for a brief moment, their images co-existing on opposite sides of the pond in unity and harmony. It was a reminder that their love was not just for themselves but for the world around them.

They traced the delicate contours of the garden's terrain. The garden, once an epitome of splendor, bore evident marks of distress. Venturing further into the garden, traces of its desolation bore whispers of the once-vibrant landscape, which was now evidently marred. The gentle blooms drooped with faded petals. The once-lush greenery wore a tired resemblance of neglect. The air carried a somber fragrance, hinting at the loss that had befallen this sacred space.

How long had they abandoned their souls? Olivette wondered. How much love had they rejected? She fervently hoped that their journey would not be in vain.

As Olivette and Nazam decided to devote their hearts and hands to the task of revival, Eve and Adam exchanged knowing glances. The desolation mirrored the challenges they had encountered in their own lives, igniting within them an unyielding determination to heal and revive this sanctuary of life and love.

The garden was divided into various sections, each holding unique elements crucial for its rejuvenation: a floral sanctum, the orchard of life, mystic ponds, enchanted groves, a rose garden, a lotus pond, and whispering meadows. The floral sanctum housed many flowers, from delicate ones to vibrant blossoms, which should glow with a burst of colors and fragrances. The orchard of life is the life source of the soul, with its abundant and succulent fruits.

Olivette clutched her chest when they came upon the mystic ponds.

"The serene waters possessed mystical abilities that could heal. The waters used to run through the garden, giving it life. We must restore it so its waters can run through the garden and bring back the rest of the garden."

Olivette looked at her chest as if she could see the parts of her that were dried up like the pond. She and Nazam could feel the flutter of hope heave within their chests. When they came upon the enchanted groves, it was silent, except for a few birds twittering weakly. The grove was supposed to shelter various fauna, nurturing the life source of the birds.

Eve chipped melodiously, "Once restored, it will thrive with the melodies of diverse birdlife."

The restoration's culmination would bring about a harmonious, thriving ecosystem within the garden, with rejuvenated life and vitality infusing every corner.

They walked through the rose garden; it was a shadow of itself. This area of the garden was once a maze of fragrant roses, but now it is a desolate place. The once-vibrant rose bushes stood forlorn: their once-lush foliage now wilted and pallid, with petals drooping in resignation. Each rose, a symbol of grace and elegance, now bore the weight of time- its colors fading into muted shades. The fragrant air, once perfumed with the sweet essence of blossoming roses, now held a faint scent tinged with melancholy. The buds that once promised to unfurl into splendid blooms now lay shriveled and unopened, deprived of the nourishment they desperately needed.

The garden path, once a picturesque walkway adorned with blooming roses on either side, now felt barren, the thorns and blemished leaves portraying a story of neglect. Despite the desolation, there remained an air of resilience, a whisper of hope lingering within the garden's forgotten beauty, waiting to be awakened by the nurturing touch of restoration.

The lotus pond was a far cry from its former charm. From glimpses in their dreams, Olivette and Nazam remembered how it mirrored the sky's complexion. It was now murky, had slits in the base, and had dead lotus flowers and leaf debris all around it. The flowers that once added beauty to the pond lay closed and faded, their petals bearing the marks of neglect. The dragonflies that used to hover above the pond had dwindled, leaving a void in the once-bustling ecosystem.

The surrounding stones and rocks appeared scattered and unkempt; the air, once filled with the soft rustling of leaves and the gentle hum of nature, was silent and smelled of dust.

"The Whispering Meadow," Adam said with the wave of his hand, gesturing towards a still expanse of land. "This place carries the wisdom of the past, present, and future. It should be an expanse of green land where the gentle winds carry the secrets of the garden. It is known to project calm and tranquility."

Yet, in the middle of this melancholy, a glimmer of hope lingered. Despite the neglect, the Lotus Pond retained an air of mystique, a silent plea for revival that awaited the healing touch of love and care.

Olivette traced her fingers lightly over the wilted petals of a once-vibrant flower, her touch tender and filled with empathy. The sight of the garden's decline stirred a mixture of sorrow and determination within her. She saw reflections of her struggles and the challenges she had faced, resonating with the garden's state of neglect. Through the desolation, she sensed a faint whisper of resilience, an indomitable spirit waiting to be rekindled.

Nazam observed the ailing plants with a sense of regret, recognizing their potential buried beneath the rubble of neglect they had administered. The garden's desolation struck a chord within him, echoing his feelings of being overlooked and misunderstood.

"I didn't know I had abandoned my soul so much." Nazam expressed his feelings of grief and shame.

Olivette and Nazam exchanged glances filled with determination, silently affirming their commitment to breathe life back into this once-glorious sanctuary. The garden's plight became a shared mission, igniting within them a collective resolve to nurture and restore not just the physical landscape but also the forgotten beauty within.

Adam directed them, his voice resonating with an air of guidance and determination. "Let's get to work," he declared, his tone a blend of authority and encouragement.

He began by dividing the tasks, recognizing the unique strengths each possessed. "Olivette will heal with her tender fingers; I suggest she dedicate herself to nurturing the fragile blooms and cultivating the garden's essence," Adam proposed, recognizing Olivette's innate ability to infuse life into the withering flora.

Eve confirmed, her voice carrying a pearl of serene wisdom that reverberated throughout the garden: "Yes, the energy coursing through her veins has given her a gift."

"She possesses a rare connection to the garden, an affinity that springs from the leaf's energy she bears within. Her touch is not merely tender; it's infused with the very essence of life itself," Eve added, acknowledging Olivette's unique connection to the garden's restorative power.

"Yes, her touch carries an unparalleled gentleness that will revive the most delicate petals. Olivette focuses on the blossoms and delicate plants. Show them the care and compassion you possess," Adam continued, highlighting Olivette's nurturing nature.

With a warm smile, Olivette accepted the task. She delved into her work with an empathetic touch, coaxing life back into wilted blooms and fragile plants. Her tender care breathed new vigor into the garden, her fingers dancing delicately through the petals, infusing them with hope and vitality. Each blossom she tended seemed to respond to her touch, gradually awakening from its dormant state.

"Perhaps you should start by tending the rose garden," he suggested, nodding towards the rose garden. "Nazam, why don't you help in clearing the debris around the lotus pond?" he added, recognizing his meticulous attention to detail.

"You're gifted at fixing things, so you will oversee structural defects. You will tend to uproot plants and replace scattered stones," Adam announced, acknowledging Nazam's eye for detail and knack for restoration.

"He'll focus on the pavilions, pathways, and any elements that need attention." Adam added, "Remember, the power is within you."

Nazam nodded, a sense of responsibility and determination gleaming in his eyes. He took charge of assessing the garden's structural integrity, noting areas that required immediate attention. With Adam's guidance, he devised plans to reinforce pathways, repair pavilions, and restore the garden's architecture, blending functionality with the garden's innate beauty. His expertise relayed the promise of the garden's revival.

As they commenced their respective tasks, Adam offered practical advice and tips, guiding them through the intricacies of nurturing the garden. He demonstrated proper techniques for pruning and caring for the plants, emphasizing the importance of patience and care in restoration. His wisdom accumulated over centuries added to his genuine desire to empower Olivette and Nazam in their restoration efforts, which reassured them.

Each stroke, each touch to the garden, was an act of renewal and rejuvenation. Olivette crouched by the rose beds, hands clasped over them as if in prayer. They labored assiduously under Adam's mentorship and with the common goal of restoring the garden's former splendor.

Nazam was methodical, his touch purposeful as he assessed the scope of repair in each area. When he encountered a cluster of wilting trees, his hands traced their weathered trunks. On contact, a subtle ripple traversed through the bark, evoking a gradual resurgence of vitality. The trees, once forlorn and weakened, responded to Nazam's touch, showing signs of renewed strength as if the very essence of life within them had been reignited.

Moving to a bed of wilted shrubs, Nazam's touch was deliberate, his palms cradling the sagging branches. With each careful movement, revitalizing energy seemed to infuse the desolate shrubbery. The wilted and curled leaves started to unfurl, their emerald color reviving as if infused with Nazam's restorative energy.

His interaction with the soil itself was pivotal; his hands cupped the dry earth, fingers sifting through the parched ground. As he infused the soil with his touch, a subtle transformation occurred. The once barren and cracked ground appeared to soften, hinting at the promise of newfound fertility as if Nazam's connection with the earth itself fostered a resurgence of life.

Nazam's touch, akin to a healer's precision, seemed to be a channel for the garden's revival. With each deliberate gesture, the landscape stirred with a subtle vibrancy, responding to his nurturing touch with a blossoming promise of restoration.

As Olivette's fingers brushed against a withered flower, a delicate tremor seemed to resonate through its wilted petals. At her touch, the flower's color, once a faded memory of its former glory, gradually began to regain its vibrant shade. The tentative opening of the petals resembled a cautious awakening as a result of Olivette's touch, which had rejuvenated them.

Moving to a patch of shriveled foliage, Olivette's fingertips traced along the desiccated leaves. With each gentle stroke, a subtle change rippled through the once-brittle foliage. The leaves, once parched and lifeless, now appeared to regain their verdant tone, a faint shimmer of vitality emerging as if responding to Olivette's healing touch.

Her next encounter was with a dormant tree, its branches barren and devoid of life. As she placed her palm against the rough bark, a faint pulse seemed to resonate beneath her touch. Gradually, buds peeked from the previously barren branches, hinting at the promise of forthcoming rejuvenation.

With each interaction, Olivette's touch seemed to catalyze a gradual revival of the garden's essence. Petal by petal and leaf by leaf, the flora came back to life thanks to the mystical power of the leaf's latent energy.

Adam and Eve watched Nazam and Olivette, deeply engrossed in their tasks. Nazam, his sleeves rolled up, meticulously assessed the damaged parts of the garden and sought ways to bring its former glory back. He was careful not to cause any damage to his work, treating his task with ardent precision and gentleness. His determination stood out, reflecting his grit and unwavering focus. Olivette, on her part, was more thoughtful, usually staying with a plant long enough to ensure it would not break with the charge of energy she lent it. Her gaze was calculating and thoughtful, each task with a strategic mindset, delicately navigating the restoration process.

For days, they toiled, watering plant after plant, with Nazam opening up blocked ridges and Olivette restoring the delicate plants. The task took four hectic days. They ate from the fruit of the small tree and slept under the shade of the old tree.

Adam and Eve exchanged glances, admiring the scene unfolding before them. They admitted that the two complemented each other well. They commended their resilience and dedication to the tasks, each one using their unique strengths towards a common goal.

While Nazam worked tirelessly within the garden's confines, he cradled his hope for the change he could bring outside the garden. His heart was set on not just reviving the garden but also on extending its restorative power to the lives waiting for him outside. His mind wandered to the thoughts of the people he could help—the possibilities of the garden's healing essence to aid those in need and to offer solace and rejuvenation to those whose lives echoed the desolation the garden had once borne.

He felt the yearning of the Holy Spirit then and prayed silently for help and guidance.

On the other hand, Olivette was thinking of the people she left at home. She envisioned herself sharing her faith outside the garden. She would spread the message of hope and renewal, carrying the transformative power she had witnessed within the garden to her community. Her determination to share the restorative power of faith burned brightly within her, and she resolved to offer a guiding light to those seeking rejuvenation amid life's desolation.

She dreamed of the towns she would visit. She anticipated meeting her aunt after everything and could almost imagine the elation that would settle on Aunt May's face when she learned about her plans.

Oh, how she missed her little Camille. Her little giggles and soft eyes.

"What are you thinking about?" Nazam appeared behind her, having finished most of his work.

"My daughter," she blushed at his exposed arms, realizing it was the first time they had talked about Camile. "You saw glimpses of her in the vision."

"Oh yes." He sat down beside her, allowing silence to settle between them.

Nazam was enamored with Olivette's nurturing demeanor and the way her touch seemed to bring life to every area of the garden during their shared journey there. He admired her empathy, her ability to infuse hope into the withered plants, and the earnestness in her eyes as she worked tirelessly to rejuvenate the garden.

"You're an exemplary mother, you know." He sighed. "A pretty young one, but a wonderful mother," he joked.

Olivette laughed. She had found herself increasingly drawn to Nazam's unwavering strength and determination. She commended the way he approached things. He had a mysterious nature, staying silent unless it was necessary to speak. She discovered she was safe with him in the short time they had known each other. *'Destiny would not intertwine my soul with a wicked one,'* she thought. She admired his gentle yet resolute nature, his resilience in the face of challenges, and the kindness he showed in the garden's restoration.

"Thank you." Olivette had grown accustomed to people instantly asking her how she made such a huge mistake. She remembered the lady on the bus and smiled sheepishly.

"It's the first time someone's called me an exemplary mother," she said, reflecting on past experiences.

"Really?" Nazam exclaimed, "Well, they don't know you like I do, do they?"

"No. They don't." Olivette felt free, a feeling she hadn't felt in a while.

Nazam looked at her with a warm smile. "Look at all the work you did here. They do not know how resilient and hardworking you are." Making animated gestures, Nazam continued, "Motherhood is like juggling flaming torches while riding a unicycle on a tightrope, right?"

Olivette chuckled, shaking her head. "Not quite that dramatic, but it's challenging, you know. I sometimes wonder if I'm doing it right."

"Oli, I believe you're doing a great job," Nazam reassured her. "Camile has a wonderful mom who cares deeply about her. Look at you juggling all this. He waved a hand towards the garden, "like a pro."

"Yeah, like trying to stop her from eating dirt and convincing her that naptime is a great idea," she said with a laugh.

Nazam nodded sympathetically. "Ah, the classic struggle. But you're rocking it, trust me."

"I appreciate that," Olivette smiled. "It's a journey, that's for sure."

"Parenting always is," Nazam replied. "But it's also a lot of fun. And you're doing splendidly, Oli." He paused, his eyes sparkling with kind curiosity. "I saw glimpses of his father in our vision. What about him?"

"He's not in the picture," Olivette replied quietly, a touch of sadness in her voice.

"It must be challenging."

"It has its moments," Olivette admitted, looking down briefly. "But Camile's my world, you know? Being a single teenage mom comes with its hurdles, but it's also rewarding." Olivette made a deliberate enunciation of 'teenage' to emphasize her point.

"He left as soon as he could." She fidgeted with her fingers. "When he told me to get rid of it, I thought he was joking because he said it with such a coy smile that I could have fooled myself into thinking I was being dramatic. After that, I avoided him because I was ashamed. How many girls of my age get pregnant? Why did it have to be me, I wondered, and with a boy who barely understood the weight of his actions?" She let the words settle between them.

"I admire your strength," Nazam said, offering her a comforting smile. "You're doing an amazing job, Oli."

"Thank you, Nazam," she replied gratefully. "It's not always easy, but Camile's worth every moment."

Their admiration for each other grew even stronger as they witnessed the garden come to life.

"*Beyond the garden, the world is vast and full of wonders, inviting us to explore, to love, and to live more fully than we ever imagined.*"

# 11

# Beyond the Garden

While Adam and Eve observed them, Olivette and Nazam looked on at the newly settled verdant patch, their eyes tracing the intricate patterns of life woven into the garden. Blooms, once wilting and faded, now shimmer with a kaleidoscope of colors. The trees swayed gently, whispering tales of revitalization, their leaves vibrant and rustling with renewed vigor.

"It's like a dream," breathed Olivette, her voice carrying the awe and wonder that enveloped them all.

Nazam nodded in agreement; his gaze drawn to the vibrant shades of color dancing before them. "I've never seen anything quite like this."

Adam and Eve exchanged serene smiles, contentment emanating from their beings as they beheld the garden's newfound radiance. "Indeed," murmured Eve, "it's just like we imagined." She looked toward Adam, silent regret resting between them.

"Even better," Adam said.

They appreciated the beauty before them, sharing a similar hope for the future.

Olivette and Nazam felt accomplished as the garden regained its vibrant state. Looking at the work they had done, they wondered how humans did not see the threads of fate connecting them beyond their differences.

"All those wars are pointless wastes of lives," Olivette said, recalling their shared vision.

"Isn't it baffling how humans are entirely oblivious to the threads of fate? Each man is so self-centered, they cannot see beyond the color of their skin or the racial differences." Nazam remarked, glancing at the garden's rejuvenated beauty.

Olivette nodded, her gaze lingering on the blossoming flora. "In the grand scheme of things, our shared struggles should matter more."

"Indeed," Nazam agreed, his eyes reflecting light from the pond. "If only more people could see beyond the surface, maybe we'd find peace."

Their conversation echoed a longing for understanding and harmony among humans, resonating with the garden's restored serenity.

Olivette turned to Nazam suddenly, a determined glint in her eyes. "We've seen it here—the power of love to heal. We have to share this with the world, Nazam."

Nazam chuckled at her animated expression. He nodded in agreement, the vision of a peaceful world reflecting in his gaze. "Olivette, we can't keep this to ourselves." He studied her face, noticing how the turmoil of her past had created fine lines around her eyes. The fine lines added to her beauty. Catching himself, Nazam shifted his weight and said, "We have to spread the message far and wide."

They sat in silent agreement, their hearts aligned in purpose. The desire to carry the garden's essence of love and restoration beyond its borders resonated deeply within them.

When they bid farewell to Adam and Eve at the garden's entrance, with their hearts filled with immense gratitude, they noticed the look of longing in Adam and Eve's eyes. Olivette and Nazam wished they could heal their broken hearts. The garden stood transformed, radiating newfound life and vitality.

Adam placed a hand on Nazam's shoulder, a silent acknowledgment passing between them. "Remember, the journey ahead is long, but now you have been equipped with far more wisdom and understanding than when you first arrived. Go forth with the light of love," he said, his voice carrying through the garden.

Eve embraced Olivette, her touch transferring an ethereal warmth to Olivette's body. "Your bond is your strength. Cherish it and let it guide you," she advised, a serene smile gracing her lips.

With a last glance at the garden, Olivette and Nazam set out on the road. They walked side by side, occasionally pausing to admire the beauty of nature or to share anecdotes from their time in the garden. Conversations echoed between them, plans taking shape as they discussed their mission, contemplating how to spread the message of love and unity. They passed by winding paths and rolling hills and experienced some moments of quiet as they ventured towards the nearest city—Mericlove.

The sun's golden rays illuminated the landscape, casting a warm glow upon the horizon.

The closer they got, the silhouette of the city gradually emerged, its spires and rooftops peeking over the horizon like a promise of new beginnings.

In the bustling yet quaint city, Olivette and Nazam found refuge from their journey. The streets were alive with vendors hawking their wares, the scent of fresh bread wafting from nearby bakeries, and the vibrant colors of handwoven fabrics on display. The inn they stumbled upon stood proudly amidst the lively thoroughfare, its wooden sign creaking softly in the breeze.

The innkeeper, a stout, and a jovial man with a warm smile, welcomed them as they entered. "Ah, weary travelers! Welcome to Mericlove," he greeted, wiping his hands on his apron. "You look like you've traveled far. Sit, sit! I'll fetch some warm soup and a place for you both to rest."

Rivers, they learned, was the innkeeper's name. He seemed to be a man of many interests—a storyteller, a bard, and a cook. He did whatever he could to serve the travelers who came by his inn.

As they settled at a table, Olivette and Nazam couldn't help but observe the diversity of the people passing by. A group of musicians strummed their instruments in a nearby corner, and Rivers would occasionally respond to the familiar tune of their music. While children played tag, their laughter echoed through the streets. There was an undeniable sense of community, an aura of simplicity and unity.

It created an atmosphere of safety and it drew travelers from many descents.

Conversations flowed between Olivette, Nazam, and the innkeeper, exchanging tales of their travels and the wonders they had seen. The innkeeper regaled them with stories of the city's history, its people, and the interconnectedness that thrived within the community.

"The city may seem small," the innkeeper remarked, wiping down the counter, "but it is a barrel of stories." His tongue rolled smoothly as he spoke, a cheerful smile masking his face. "People from all walks of life take refuge here."

Olivette and Nazam nodded, feeling the magnetic pull of the place—the perfect setting to begin their mission of sharing love and understanding among people, starting with this warm and welcoming city.

They asked for rooms to lay their heads and the innkeeper led them up the stairs that led to the top of the restaurant. The inn is a quaint establishment nestled at the edge of the city, made of wooden doors. When they reached the floor above the restaurant, they met the innkeeper's sister, a middle-aged woman with a welcoming smile. She rose as soon as she saw the guests, bustling about attending to them.

"Hey Mary," the innkeeper regarded her with a familiar smile, their resemblance obvious by their hazel streaks of hair. Olivette was greeted with a polite nod, her voice carrying a gentle warmth. "My name is Olivette."

"Nazam here." Nazam waved a hand at Mary.

The next day, after breakfast, they set about sharing their message of hope, starting with the innkeeper.

Olivette met the innkeeper with his sister at the reception and said, "Good morning."

"Hey there. Sleep well?"

"Yes. I am just so eager to share the message from my travels. I have a message of hope and restoration that I'd like to share."

Mary, wiping her hands on her apron, regarded Olivette curiously. "Hope and restoration, you say? I want to hear all about it."

"We've uniquely experienced the power of love, and we believe it holds the key to healing and unity," Olivette explained, her eyes alight with conviction. "We've seen it firsthand in a garden that was once desolate but has now been restored to its former glory."

The innkeeper's curiosity piqued, his gaze glimmering with interest and skepticism. "Love restoring a garden? I've heard many tales, but this one seems quite extraordinary."

"It is," affirmed Olivette. "We believe it's a message worth sharing, especially in a world where division and strife often cloud our vision of unity and understanding."

The innkeeper leaned in, intrigued. "Tell me more, dear. Sit down and share your story with me."

As she described their journey, the transformative power they had seen, and the hope they held for a world filled with love's healing energy, Olivette sat down by the fireplace. As she spoke, Rivers and Mary listened intently, absorbing every word with a mix of wonder and contemplation.

Gathered around a worn wooden table in a corner of the inn, Olivette and Nazam found a group of travelers and went to speak with them. They shared their experiences, the journey from the desolate garden to the city, and the transformative power of love they had witnessed.

"We've seen miracles happen when love guides our actions," Olivette explained, her voice resonating with conviction. "The garden we restored stands as a testament to the healing potential within each of us."

One of the travelers, a weathered man with a kind smile, leaned forward. "A garden brought back to life by love? That's quite a tale," he said, disbelief dotting his words.

"We hope to inspire others to believe in the strength of love." Without missing a beat, Nazam chimed in, his gaze earnest. "We're not on a mission to change the world overnight, but to plant seeds of hope that can bloom into something greater."

The travelers' tale piqued their interest, and they exchanged curious glances. They talked about their journeys, sharing moments of despair and hope. As the evening wore on, the air in the inn became charged with a sense of shared purpose and possibility.

One of them spoke up. "Perhaps our paths will intertwine again. If love truly holds such power, it's a message worth carrying to every corner of this world."

Olivette and Nazam nodded, smiling at the thought. They both vowed to carry forward the message of love and restoration in their travels, spreading hope wherever their journeys took them.

They stayed at Mariclove for two days, sharing the message with as many travelers as they could find. When it was time to leave, the innkeeper gave them food for the rest of the journey, thankful for the message of hope and love they had brought to his doorstep.

The morning sun painted the sky with hues of amber as Nazam and Olivette stood at the edge of the town, ready to embark on their separate paths. Their eyes held a shared understanding, a silent acknowledgment of the bond they had shared during their journey.

"Until we meet again." Nazam's voice carried a sense of hope as he smiled at Olivette, his gaze filled with unspoken gratitude.

"Take care, Nazam," Olivette replied, her tone laced with a hint of wistfulness. "Thank you for everything."

They would hold on to the memories and remember their shared encounters in the garden. They exchanged a last embrace, a bittersweet farewell filled with the promise of future encounters.

As they parted ways, a sense of determination coursed through each of them. They carried with them the lessons learned, the wisdom gained, and the shared vision of spreading love and understanding in a world often fraught with discord.

The town slowly faded into the distance behind Olivette as she embarked on her next adventure. Her heart was filled with gratitude for the friendships formed and the experiences that had shaped her.

# 12

# Unveiling the Treasures Within

Days passed and Olivette trudged the rest of the way alone. However, this time, the road she took was shorter and with more kind people. Olivette did not wonder why the leaf had taken her through such a long road when she could have taken a shorter route. She understood that the ordeals she had faced on the way to the garden were necessary.

As Olivette approached her house, her heart pounded with a mix of anticipation and relief. As she pushed open the familiar door, the warmth of home enveloped her. Her mother stood in the hallway, her eyes brimming with unspoken emotions.

"Olivette!" Her mother's voice quivered slightly, the words catching in her throat as she enveloped her daughter in a tight embrace. The years had etched a trace of worry lines on her mother's face. She had faced so many challenges, none that Olivette could imagine, and in this embrace, she developed a new sense of admiration for her mother.

"I missed you, Mom," Olivette murmured, holding back tears, overcome by her mother's love. Her mother's touch was soothing, a reminder of the unconditional support she was willing to give her.

"You're back, safe and sound." Her mother pulled back slightly, holding Olivette's face in her hands, studying her features as if to ensure she was real and unharmed. "Tell me everything. How was your journey?"

Olivette's eyes sparkled with enthusiasm, eager to recount the details of her pilgrimage. She had grown in wisdom on her journey and as she recounted her experiences, her mother listened intently, pride evident in her eyes. The two shared laughter and tears, reminiscing while eagerly embracing the present moment.

"I'm so glad you're back, my dear," her mother said, a smile playing at the corners of her lips. "You've grown in ways I can't even imagine. You've made us proud."

"Your father would be so proud of you." This brought fresh tears to Olivette's eyes. She wondered what he would say to her at this moment. She missed him so much.

Once settled in the cozy living room, the fireplace crackling softly, Olivette and her mother exchanged knowing glances, brimming with unspoken questions and the weight of experiences from their time apart.

"Where do I even begin?" Olivette sighed, feeling a rush of emotions bubbling within her. "So much has happened, Mom."

Her mother nodded, her eyes fixed on Olivette, silently urging her to share.

"This journey has changed everything," Olivette started, her voice filled with a mixture of trepidation and excitement. "I see things more clearly. I feel something has changed within me. I feel... whole."

Her mother listened attentively, as Olivette recounted the magical encounters, the challenges faced, and the profound lessons learned during her odyssey. She shared the stories of the garden, their encounter with Adam and Eve, their realization of love's transformative power, and their quest to spread its message.

"I discovered parts of myself I never knew existed; parts of me that I had abandoned," Olivette confessed, her eyes shimmering with new-found wisdom and a touch of vulnerability.

Her mother smiled warmly, with a glimmer of pride in her eyes. "You've grown, my dear. Your journey has left its mark on you, and I can see the strength it has brought you."

Their conversation flowed into the night, blending stories of the past with hopes for the future. Olivette found solace in her mother's arms. Resting her head on her mother's shoulders, she felt reassured that even after such an extraordinary journey, their love and connection for each other remained—a love she willfully ignored in the past. She had now learned that love could change everything. She looked at her mother in a new light, appreciating all her efforts and understanding her better than before.

Olivette's mother tightened her embrace, planting a kiss on Olivette's forehead. Her eyes sparkled with quiet joy. "I always believed this day would come and that you'd find this beautiful part of yourself. You've always had a remarkable spirit, Olivette."

A warmth spread through Olivette's chest, grateful for her mother's unwavering support. "Thank you, Mom. I'm so glad to be back home with you."

"We should go to church this Sunday," her mother suggested with a smile. "It's been a while since we've gone together."

"Oh yes, that sounds perfect."

"I'm looking forward to it."

Olivette nodded, a sense of peace settling within her. "Oh, it'll be good to be back in the familiar pews."

As they continued talking, Olivette allowed herself to sink into her mother's embrace even more. She felt so content for the first time in years. She felt a sense of belonging and realized just how much she'd been pushing everyone away.

When she began to talk about Nazam, her eyes lit, animated with memories of their shared moments.

Her mother noticed the sparkle in Olivette's eyes as she spoke about Nazam. "He sounds like a wonderful person," her mother commented, observing the subtle shift in her daughter's demeanor.

"He is," Olivette replied, a soft smile gracing her lips. "We've been through so much together. He's kind, brave, and has a heart full of compassion."

Her mother chuckled gently. "Sounds like someone special. Will you see him again?"

"We promised we would," Olivette said wistfully. "We might take different paths for now, but we'll meet again someday. Also, I don't think the threads of fate are finished with us yet."

Her mother nodded. "Some connections are meant to endure, no matter where life takes you. It's a beautiful feeling to share such a connection."

Just then, they were interrupted by Camile's sudden cries, jolting both women from their positions.

Olivette's heart clenched at the sound, and she rushed to Camile's side. As she scooped her up, her cries softened into hiccupping sobs against her shoulder. Tears welled up in Olivette's eyes, but they weren't tears of sorrow or despair. They were tears of joy and hope.

"She's scared," Olivette murmured, trying to soothe Camile as she held her close. Joining her, Camile's mother provided gentle back rubs and offered comforting words.

Olivette's voice, filled with unspoken emotion, whispered, "I've got you, my sweet girl. Despite shedding tears, she embraced her new-found belief with gratitude. With a sense of renewed strength, she recognized her untapped potential to support Camile.

As Olivette cradled Camile, comforting him with tenderness, her mother observed the scene with a knowing look. Tears welled up in her eyes, reflecting a deep understanding of the transformation she witnessed in her daughter. She saw the strength and resilience that Olivette had developed.

Unable to contain her emotions, Olivette's mother approached and gently placed a hand on her daughter's shoulder. "Oh, dear," she whispered, her voice quivering with a mix of pride and empathy. "You've grown so much, and I am so proud of you."

Tears trickled down her mother's cheeks as she felt the weight of the experiences that had reshaped Olivette. There was a silent acknowledgment between them, a shared understanding of the trials that had led to this transformation.

"Oh! yes," she remembered. She had to inform Olivette's aunt of the recent development. She dialed Aunt May's number. As soon as she picked up, the distance seemed to melt away as they exchanged heartfelt greetings, their voices carrying warmth and familiarity.

"Oli's back home," Olivette's mother said, her tone brimming with emotion. "You should hear all the things she has to say."

"Oh, Oli dear." Aunt May's excited voice echoed through the speaker, and Olivette's mother recounted an abbreviated version of Olivette's experience.

She listened intently to Aunt May's responses, the conversation evolving into a beautiful exchange of insights and experiences. They spoke of love's transformative power and the significance of nurturing relationships through conscious effort.

Over the phone, the three women found unity in their understanding of love's depth, recognizing its capacity to shape and enrich their lives.

# 13

# *The Dance of Love*

In the days that followed, Olivette developed a deep sense of satisfaction for the gift of friendship. She was thankful for her mother, her aunt, and Camile—all the people God had placed in her life.

On a bright Saturday afternoon, as the sun filtered in through the clouds, Olivette sat in her room, the memories of her past flashing like fragments of a distant dream. She compared the shadows of her past to the light that showered on her life now. The contrast was striking.

Her past was a veil that limited her. It was a period of struggles, errors, and the weight of secrets. Darkness persisted in every nook and cranny of her mind and her heart felt heavy with unspoken pain and unanswered questions.

The present, however, was a picture adorned with colors she hadn't known before—bright and hopeful. Love had woven its way into the fabric of her existence, unraveling the knots of despair and fear that had bound her. It was a time of healing, forging meaningful connections, and discovering the profound depth of the human spirit.

Reminiscing, Olivette commended herself for her growth. She had shed the weight of past sorrows, embracing the lessons learned and nurturing the seeds of newfound wisdom. Her journey had sculpted her into a person she would not have recognized in the past—a person filled with resilience, empathy, and an unwavering belief in the power of love.

Camile's laughter filled the house, reminding Olivette of the joy she brought into her world. As she watched her sleep, her thoughts danced between the past and the present, contrasting the memories of her journey to this point.

The phone calls with Nazam were a lifeline, a bridge that connected them as they navigated the twists and turns of life's dance. Each call felt like a shared journey through their pasts, building a foundation for the present and potentially the future.

Despite not being Camile's father, Nazam was kind to Camile. Their talks ranged from everyday things to discussions about life's complexities, strengthening their connection and shared aspirations. They spoke of their dreams and shared an unspoken understanding of their bond.

As Camile continued to dream in the quietude of the night, Olivette's phone buzzed again, signaling another call from Nazam. These conversations were more than mere words; they were threads weaving together: shared moments, hopes, and the realization that love could span the distance between them.

In these moments of reflection, she acknowledged that love could change anything. No matter how broken one is, love heals.

# CONCLUSION

As we conclude Olivette and Nazam's tale, their journey is entwined with a powerful narrative of love, resilience, and self-discovery. Their story illustrates the enduring strength of love and the transformative journey of the human spirit.

Olivette's narrative reflects resilience, growth, and an unyielding belief in the transformative power of love. Navigating through memories, she realized her journey wasn't just about physical distance but a soulful odyssey, unraveling the intricate layers of her existence.

The dance floor became Olivette's refuge, a place to release life's burdens and embrace a carefree spirit, reminding us that joy can be found amidst life's trials. Stepping onto that vibrant dance floor sparked a sense of new beginnings, initiating her transformation. At the journey's end, Olivette embraced her changed life, blending her past with the present and sowing seeds for an unknown future.

Through her love for her daughter, Olivette discovered that love transcends boundaries, possessing the power to heal wounds and unite disparate souls. Her discussions with Nazam sparked a transformation, forming a timeless connection through shared dreams and understanding and guiding them through challenges toward new beginnings.

Her journey, relatable to many at their crossroads, renewed her vibrancy after encountering Adam and Eve in the Garden of Eden. This renewal strengthened her belief in restoration and love, guided by faith and the Holy Spirit.

Olivette's story questions our perception of the world, prompting a reflection on our families and the surrounding people. It offers hope, reminding us that love is an inner treasure waiting to be unearthed—a guiding force in our lives.

Beyond the garden, Olivette and Nazam continue their journey, inspiring hope and self-discovery across diverse landscapes. They advocate spreading love's wisdom gained from their experiences, urging others to embark on their paths of love and compassion.

In the pages unveiled, we've witnessed love transcending boundaries, resilience overcoming adversity, and the pursuit of self-discovery. "Dancing in Darkness" urges us to embrace love's dance in our lives, uncover hidden treasures within, and share transformative love.

As we conclude this extraordinary journey, let's remember that love binds us all, illuminating even the darkest paths. Olivette's tale encourages us to embrace our hearts' rhythms, seek inner treasures, and spread love's healing power.

As we close "Dancing in Darkness," let's carry its message forward. Love is our strength and guiding light—an eternal quest for self-discovery. Embrace your unique dance, allowing love to illuminate and unite us all.

The dance of love continues beyond this final chapter. May the message reshape our perception; letting love be our guiding light and eternal pursuit. Embrace your dance and illuminate the world with love and self-discovery.

**The Theme Song for Dancing in Darkness**

"What would you do, if He walked into the room?"

(live)

By Elevation Worship.

# ABOUT THE AUTHOR

Jerushia McDonald, a mother and international best-selling author, along with her daughter, Patrina Wisdom, was appointed a Global Peace Ambassador by Reverend Sun Moon of the Unification Church. She has taken the nec-essary strides to fulfill that role. She started her non-profit organization: Women with a Vision International in 1989. Jerushia spoke to people of different ages, nationalities, religious backgrounds, and co-operate groups. This transitioned to 'Africans Cry' in 2001, with a mission to unite, heal, atone, and celebrate Africans in the Diaspora. It is now known as the 'Global United Voices Network'(G.U.V.N.), initially created to bridge the gap and build peace among all nations and tongues.

Jerushia, a self-promoter, travels worldwide, documenting her journey and spreading peace among the people she encounters. She has been honored to speak on platforms around the world to various leaders of faith while building bridges of peace for future generations.

A native of Las Vegas, NV, and a single mother at 16, Jerushia started her life working in various hotels in Las Vegas before moving to New York for better opportunities for herself and her daughter, Patrina. Jerushia launched into the fashion world and entertainment industry, performing with her siblings in a small band called McDonald Five. She became a print and fashion model, becoming the First African American full-figured in the 80's model to appear in Vogue, Essence, and Ebony Magazines, and various catalogs. Also, she appeared on shows like the Oprah Winfrey Show, Phil Donahue Show, Good Morning America, and so on.

Her experiences and the challenges on her spiritual journey have kept her on the path of production on radio, conferences, and TV. Jerushia believes that the events in her life were intentional and part of her journey; gracefully relying on her faith and experiences to overcome any adversity she faces. She is excited to share more details about her plans, which extend beyond traveling.

Jerushia is working on writing three books. The first is "Dancing in Darkness: A Teenage Mother's Journey of Resilience, Self-Discovery, and Love." A Disney and Avatar feel, awakening the true image of women. Her second book, "Evolving Women" highlights the steps of a woman's journey into spirituality and self-unity. The third book, "Black Cross" examines the experiences of slave women and their descendants, how they connect to the Creator, and ultimately empowered to bless their families and communities.

Jerushia emphasizes the importance of being mindful of the challenges that come with "doing what we do to let go and move onto the next phase of life when it's our time." Recognized for her peace efforts, she has received the key to the city of Cincinnati, Ohio, for coordinating and leading a peace rally and serving as a mentor, volunteer, board member, and community activist. She plans to continue extending herself to youth, men, and women from all walks of life.

Additionally, she aims to continue using technology to build bridges by establishing her own production company in radio and television. She is currently working on relaunching "The Wrapping with Mama Rue," a talk show in the form of a series, featuring a mother's touch of life's wisdom learned, scriptural foundations, and testimonies from women with various backgrounds. The show aims to present content on entrepreneurs, women and their visions, health, family, careers, and more. She also plans to include men in her talk show with dialogue or open mic sessions on the topic 'Adam's viewpoint on Returning to the Garden.'

Having traveled to various countries, including Kenya, South Africa, North Korea, Switzerland, Nepal, Bali, Thailand, Malaysia, and The United States of America, Jerushia feels that each journey she undertakes births something deeper, demonstrating that where there is unity, there is power.

Website: https://nwlvfs.com
Instagram: @Jerushia_unscripted_unplugged

www.ingramcontent.com/pod-product-compliance
Lightning Source LLC
Chambersburg PA
CBHW050513160726
48003CB00001B/283